CE

ON THE BEGINNING OF SOCIAL INQUIRY

ON THE BEGINNING
OF SOCIAL INQUIRY

Peter McHugh   *York University, Toronto*

Stanley Raffel   *University of Edinburgh*

Daniel C. Foss   *Montclair State College, New Jersey*

Alan F. Blum   *York University, Toronto*

ROUTLEDGE & KEGAN PAUL
London and Boston

First published in 1974
by Routledge & Kegan Paul Ltd
Broadway House, 68–74 Carter Lane,
London EC4V 5EL and
9 Park Street,
Boston, Mass. 02108, U.S.A.

Printed in Great Britain by
Clarke, Doble & Brendon Ltd, Plymouth

ISBN 0 7100 77653 (C)
0 7100 77661 (P)

Library of Congress Catalog Card Number 73–89199

CONTENTS

1 INTRODUCTION

This book is a treatment of certain important ideas in sociology and social science, among them positivism, art, and common sense. But it is also a collaboration, and it would be best to introduce our work with this fact because, although it is not to be found in the table of contents, our collaboration is as much responsible for this book as any of the topics which appear there. Just as it is our conception of sociological analysis that has produced these topics, so also does our conception of analysis make collaboration a necessity and not a happenstance.

The way we work together must be distinguished from the usual master–disciple affiliations, to begin with, as well as from the tactical and temporary formation of united fronts. These are arrangements in which the decision to collaborate is transparently political, intended to broaden the reception and scope of an ambitious theory, and their purely political character may explain why they often go badly, why masters overshadow or split with disciples, why united fronts never last.

Neither is our collaboration to be identified with the component divisions of labour that originate in different training, ability, interests, and, alas, even in plain lack of energy. Such origins can only become associations of convenience: they permit the many to do 'more' than the one can do, there being no particular reason for the teamwork except dissatisfaction with individual limitations. The result is that members of the 'team' are almost always distinguishable. Ideas can 'belong' to one person as against another and the extent of each 'contribution' can be assessed. If this is what is meant by a team, then our kind of collaboration must be distinguished from teamwork. We do not, indeed cannot, differentiate among ourselves in that way.

Another collaborative rationale is that it is more effective than working alone; that two heads are better than one. For us, however, it is not just that collaboration is effective but that it is necessary. We claim that our ideas—our theory if you like—makes collaboration necessary, and not merely that collaboration produced our ideas (although that is true, too). Instead of two heads being better than one, we maintain that the notion of a head requires at least two participants. This, of course, is to suggest again that our conception of sociology is different from conventional ones which consider collaboration unnecessary or even unnatural. What, then, is our conception of analysis such that collaboration becomes a necessity?

Analysis depends on that which enables it to be done in any case, not on the contingent description which, as product, serves to obscure its origins. Analysis, for us, is generative. It is not finding something in the world, or making sense of some puzzling datum, or answering an interesting question, or locating a phenomenon worthy of study, or resolving a long-standing disagreement or any other essentially empirical procedure. To analyse is, instead, to address the possibility of *any* finding, puzzle, sense, resolution, answer, interest, location, phenomenon, etcetera, etcetera. Analysis is the concern not with anything said or written but with the grounds of whatever is said—the foundations that make what is said possible, sensible, conceivable. For any speech, including, of course, speech about speech, our interest is reflexive. For the analyst any speech, including his own, is of interest not in terms of what it says but in terms of how what it says is possible, sensible, rational in the first place. Our interest in what we call the grounds or auspices

2

of phenomena rather than in the phenomena themselves is exemplified in every chapter in this volume. To analyse the subject of research bias, for example, we do not identify instances or propose remedies. Instead we try to show the deep auspices—positivism in this case—which make sensible any actual charge of bias or any urge to remedy it. Similarly, snubs become for us not a kind of behaviour that goes on between persons in the real world, but a version of common sense which makes it conceivable that snubs would be seeable at all.

So an interest in analysis is an interest in auspices. But we should be careful to note that our interest is not exhausted by 'locating' the origins in the world of bias, art, snubs, evaluation, motives or any other topic. That we can do such locating is in itself of interest only if it directs attention not simply to descriptions of bias or snubs, but to what makes it possible for us to have produced those descriptions in the first place, i.e., to our auspices, and therefore to what, as it were, makes us possible as well. This is no easy matter.

It is no easy matter as a consequence of the act of writing. Again according to our conception of analysis, collaboration is necessary because to write is to lose one's grasp of auspices by attempting to formulate them: to write is to forget why you write; to be caught up in the activity of formulation is to face away from one's own fundamental grounds through which those formulations come about. Collaborators (others) are occasions for recollecting that grasp: others help us to remember. Our bad memories are not a weakness. They (like collaboration) are made necessary by our auspices. Since we treat every finding, every speech, every chapter in this book as mere surface reflection of what makes them possible, since no speech is in this sense perfect or self-sufficient, speaking and writing is always from the perspective of analysis an inadequate activity. In being done it always makes available for analysis a new problem, namely how *it* is possible. Speech never 'solves' this problem, if by solve is meant to remedy, because any imaginable solution (any new speech) is itself a new version of the same old problem. Yet we speak. In speaking we are denying that we are doing an inadequate activity. Otherwise our speech would be no different than chatter, than silence, than what Rosen calls nihilism.[1] In

[1] Stanley Rosen, *Nihilism: A Philosophical Essay*, New Haven Yale: University Press, 1969.

denying the inadequacy of speech in order to speak, we are denying our own auspices. This is where collaborators come in. They serve to formulate for us the inadequacy of our speech by showing how it is a surface reflection of our auspices. By formulating our speech they allow us to be committed both to speaking *and* to the reflexive character of analysis. Collaborators remind us of that which we have to forget in order to speak. Without collaborators we would either have no reason to speak, because to speak would deny our auspices, or else we would have to give up our commitment to analysis.

One way to formulate our collaboration is through the standard terms of ego and alter. Ego, for us, is the speaker who, by speaking, necessarily forgets his reason for speech. Alter reminds ego why he speaks by formulating ego's auspices. We conceive ego then to make reference to his auspices in order that alter may formulate them. In this way, alter makes it rational for ego to speak. Conceiving of both ego and alter together, which is to say conceiving of collaboration, is our method for being able to produce an analysis which is reflexive, which addresses its own possibilities, and yet is at the same time speakable, do-able, distinct from chatter, a denial of nihilism. Alter and ego collaborate to generate analysis.

This view of ego and alter and how, together, they can do analysis is, of course, only a promissory formulation at this point. We shall make reference to the idea again and again throughout this book. Our immediate interest is in the writing of this book, which forced us to create a concrete format consistent with that analytic notion. The method we hit upon, after various false starts, is one which involves several distinct phases of work. The first step is for one of us to write up some of our material (even before this stage, however, there has been extensive interchange in working the ideas up to the point where they can be written about). When a paper has been produced, it becomes grist for our mill. Everyone writes a response in the form of another whole and self-contained paper (not just a set of notes or suggestions). These responses are distributed to the whole group and they are discussed, in conjunction with the original. Then someone edits the full collection of material into a 'finished' paper. These 'finished' papers constitute this book.

How does this format relate to our idea of collaborating? The original paper can be thought of as ego and the responses

4

as alter. This is to suggest that the responses are not criticisms as that term is ordinarily used. They should neither praise nor blame the original. Nor do they accept or reject it in the way scientific gatekeepers do. They do not make the kind of 'comments' with which colleagues greet most academic papers. However appropriate they may be in other contexts, such comments serve to emphasise the difference between writer and commentator as between the one who is answerable to the other, rather than as the two who collaborate. In this respect, the critical function of ordinary evaluation serves to mark and reinforce differentiated individual responsibility for a paper and in so doing marks and reinforces the distinction between criticism and collaboration. The point for us, however, is not to differentiate the second group of writers from the first in terms of such differentiated responsibility, or by citing different ability, interests, opinions, or whatever. Instead, the response papers seek to enter into relationship with the original by transforming its present but unexplicated features. They are alters to the originals' egos. Second papers formulate for the originals the auspices under which the latter were produced.

In one respect, second papers should always be deeper than first. But not because the response writers are cleverer or even because science marches on. Second papers are deeper than first by their very nature. The fact of a first paper makes possible a second which formulates the auspices of the first.

The editor in our scheme, whose job it is to assemble a finished paper, does not merely separate the wheat from the chaff. Although second papers will be deeper than first, they do not make first papers obsolete. Like alters, second papers are only sensible in terms of the ego to which they are responding. Therefore the finished paper will include material from both the original and the responses to it. For example, the paper on snubs includes both a description of what snubs are and, then, a version of how that description is possible in the first place. The paper on evaluation begins with descriptions of theoretical problems not so that we can later pose solutions but to enable us to suggest later what makes it possible to see these as problems to begin with. All papers include ideas which are, in the course of the papers themselves, deepened.

If we can deepen, one might ask, why include the superficial material at all? Because it is the 'superficial' material which makes possible its own deepening. We are not in the position of the desperate comedian whose poor material produces a half hour of duds for 15 minutes of laughs. We are more like the playwright for whom the clarity of the third act requires the confusion of the first and second. Instead of selecting out the right from the wrong, or the good from the bad, our editors must attempt to display the dynamics of the relationship between the original and the response, between the speech and its possibility, between ego and alter. Notice an interesting general implication. We cannot accept the conventional recommendation that a science should forget its founders. Rather we remember our founders, which is to say we try to remember why they speak.

Having given an account of how our concrete format of original paper, response, and edit relates to our idea of collaboration and analysis, we must now enter a caveat which is really a general principle of our entire project. While our format may have a certain consistency with our analytic notions, it cannot stand to our theoretical ideas as a building to its blueprint. Ego and alter as we formulate them can only be imperfectly realised in actual situations. An original paper is never a concretely perfect ego. Some originals cannot be responded to. Others formulate themselves to some extent, which is to say they do the work of both ego and alter. Similarly, some responses seem irrelevant to the original. Other responses are more useful egos than alters. Sometimes we have to throw away material. Often we give up on some material in midstream. Our procedures, in spite of their theoretical grounding, are *ad hoc* rather than invariant.

We 'admit' to this flexibility, this practicality in our actual work, not just because we are honest, but because it is not for us a damaging admission. We are not even in the position of those sociologists at work who more or less reluctantly confess the discrepancy between the ideal and actual. Instead we insist that the idea of analysis requires, without exception, a distinction between the concrete character of situations and the theoretical scheme. It is not that the harsh realities of the real world force us to abandon utopian bromides like ego and alter and even collaboration, but that in so far as ego and alter and collaboration are serious ideas there can be nothing that 'corresponds' to them in the real world. There are many examples of this point in the papers that follow: we suggest that motives are not states belonging to persons but are an observer's method for generating the idea of person. We show how bias is not, for us, a thing in the world, but a method for making that thing available. Similarly, art conceived analytically is not a distinct group of objects but a way of seeing any object. Our procedure is never to do a description of what actually is the case but rather to generate for any potential description—motives, bias, art, snubs, evaluation—the deep grounds which make it sensible.

If our format—our method of collaborating—represents our version of rational discourse, then we must say that, as we conceive of theorising, the theorist cannot produce a set of standard rules which, if followed, will lead to actual discourse that is rational. Analysis, as we practise it, is concerned with constructing for any behaviour its rationality, but not with producing rational behaviour. Theorists like Skinner and Habermas, who try to generate good talk in the real world by means of theoretical schemes, are really failing to distinguish behaviour and analysis. Our position is closer to Chomsky's. To commit oneself to programming the real world is to give up on theorising. Therefore, the fact that our actual practices are *ad hoc*, variable, only more or less successful, is not a disappointment but rather an affirmation of the distinction we make between analysis and behaviour.

Let's summarise the points we have made so far. First we suggested that our conception of analysis—analysis which is reflexive and yet can be spoken—requires collaboration. By this we meant that it requires an ego who speaks and thereby denies his auspices and an alter who formulates the auspices ego forgets by speaking. Then, we suggested how our format is consistent with our analytic notion in that original papers are like egos, responses are like alters, and editing portrays the relationship between ego and alter. However, we stressed that the idea of collaboration does not have a strict correspondence to our actual practices, which have to be *ad hoc*. Now we want to pursue one implication of this last point: no set of actual practices can ever exhaust the idea of collaboration. The simple reason for this is that alter, by speaking, by formulating ego's auspices, becomes an ego in his own right. This is to say that our response writers, even if they can be seen as alters to the original papers' egos, become egos simply by writing responses. Any actual formulation of ego by alter can raise the same problem which it solves, namely how *it* is possible. To raise the problem is in our terms to transform alter's formulation of ego's auspices itself into an account that needs auspices—to transform alter, in other words, into an ego such that the latter needs to be grounded. This is a logic in which collaboration need not stop when a paper, for example a paper in this book, is produced. We have collaborated in ego–alter fashion, and now we ask that the reader collaborate in the same way. The papers in this book should be conceived of as displays which require alters. This is where readers come in. Readers are asked to treat our papers reflexively. They are asked to become our collaborators. This is our version of how to read.

The fact that we want and need collaboration from our readers is one reason why we do not like to consider our papers finished in the usual sense of the word. All our papers are essentially open-ended in that the very method they use, namely formulating auspices, can be applied to them. This frees the reader to do things with the material which are not available in studies based on other conceptions of author and reader. Most social-scientific work typically depends upon whether the author can convince you that his descriptions are correct. This dependency results from a conception of author and reader as mutually substitutable observers with identical access to a world. They do not distinguish author and reader as ego and alter in the way we do, which means that the acceptability of their work is contingent upon its reception as nothing more than a report, a report which might have issued from *either* party, whether author *or* reader. It is this conception which limits the reader to an assessment of correctness, because he must act in this scheme of mutual substitutability to exactly reproduce the author and no more—if he can reproduce the author, his assessment is that the report is correct. If not, the report must be thought not correct. We, on the other hand, do not depend for cogency upon whether our descriptions of snubs and bias and the rest are correct by convincing you that we are mutually substitutable. Because participation by the reader is differentiated in our case according to the differentiated relation between ego and alter, we can anticipate and hope that we are 'only' providing a way of seeing these concrete affairs such that you could see those affairs in some grounded way, not necessarily

8

in just the way we do. These are papers which seek a conversation, as it were. In other words, we hope by providing our auspices to enable you, the reader, to see snubs and bias dialectically: by taking on the collaborative role of alter, you can formulate the auspices that lead you to see how it is *possible* that they come to look like whatever they look like.

Another important matter is the status of the phrase 'unfinished work'. That our papers are not finished does not distinguish them from other pieces of sociology. Rather, the difference is that our incompleteness is grounded whereas theirs is treated as happenstance. Consider for example one notion of the future of functional analysis. Committed functionalists will often acknowledge that functionalism has flaws. However, these flaws (a kind of incompleteness) are treated as things to be repaired if only. . . . If only functionalists had the wit, the experience, the foresight, or especially the money. The future for these people becomes the time—sooner or later—when the money will accumulate and temporary failures become permanent successes. Failures are nothing to worry about because, by the nature of the case, they are temporary. A theory has defects only because the theorist happens to be situated in time and space, in an economic structure. This relativisation to the conditions of failure is a perfect method for managing in a Goffmanesque sense, but it hardly comes to grips with the trouble. By anticipating termination, they think their work will come to have a final character, in the way that what is final is the equivalent of what is successful. They are oriented to the possibility of closure and it is in terms of this that they measure success and failure. We say, on the contrary, that our work, because of the nature of analysis, will always be in need of repair, whether successful or not.

It follows from the different methods which we and the functionalists have for seeing our incompleteness—for us the inevitable consequence of reflexivity, for them the circumstantial contingency—that we will also have different ideas about how our work should be read. For functionalist formulations of the ideal reader, see any one of their introductions. Perhaps the key to reading them as they would like to be read is patience. They ask readers to treat instances (their failures) as footsteps on the stairway to permanent success. Reading our papers as we would like them to be read involves seeing their *essential* incompleteness. This essential incompleteness is grounded in our conception of analysis and in the fact that the idea of collaboration cannot be exhausted by any actual paper nor any actual reader. Needless to say, seeing a paper's essential incompleteness is a different matter from finding some papers to be shorter than they should be, or some ideas to be inadequately expressed. We ask our readers to collaborate by using the papers to grasp the reason for the essential incompleteness, which is to say we ask them to grasp the conception of analysis which makes the papers possible. The papers themselves are never the point, although they have to be used to make the point.

The papers should be read as *examples* of our method. This is not to say that, like most books, we use many examples. Rather, the whole book is an example. The book (and each paper) is an exemplification of that which makes it possible. It is ego's attempt to make reference to his auspices so that alter (reader) can formulate those auspices. Every last word is meant to do this work of exemplifying. Examples in our sense should not be confused with data. They do not refer to the world—they are not descriptions. They are more like icons. They should be used to refer back to what makes them possible—to our conception of analysis. Our examples are not imperfect if by that is meant they could be improved upon. We are not in the position of the would-be researcher settling for examples until he can get another grant. We have to use examples. They are the sole way we can speak because, in writing, we can only attend to the formulable or exemplifiable side of reflexivity. Here we are reintroducing the same issue we developed earlier to explain why we have to collaborate. Speech, except by example, would have to be perfect speech. Only if one could imagine a speech which speaks auspices without creating the same reflexive problem it solves could one imagine anything but speech by examples. As we have already said, we cannot imagine perfect speech. Example, then, is our version of how alter can formulate the essential imperfection and yet the usability of ego's speech. Example is to say the speech is imperfect because it does not speak its own auspices but usable because it allows alter to formulate its auspices.

As we use it, the notion of everyday life has the analytic

10

status of an example. Rather than refer to everyday life as the 'rockbottom' certainty to which our descriptions purport to correspond, such a notion of everyday life is itself a construction. We use it as the point of reference for the conventions of speech and usage with which we begin our analyses. Everyday life is the source of the examples with which we begin and it acquires its analytic status for us as an example; everyday life serves as the exemplification of the beginning of analysis in its conventions of speech and usage. Yet, our use of everyday life is distinguished from all other prevailing uses through our conception of this beginning as itself a result or achievement. Thus, everyday life as the example typifies the concerted tendency of analysis to begin with some 'matter' securely in hand. Our analysis then seeks to dissolve what is in hand by treating the security of the example as covering over and concealing its history.

In a way then, our analyses are directed to the history of everyday life, if by that it is understood that examples serve to alert us to the ways in which the conventions of ordinary thought have become segregated from their grammatical grounds. Whereas 'history' suggests for us the character of such grounds, 'everyday life' typifies any and all of the occasions of thought and action which we decide to take as a point of departure for historical analysis.

Everyday life is then not a phenomenon but an impetus; it provides the practical and concrete incentive for reflexive inquiry. In itself, it does not pose the problem of 'data' which invite an account; rather, being a reminder of the way in which the ordinary has become forgetful of its history, it serves to exercise our analytic wit to re-collect and to re-think this history. If as Mallarmé says, 'the word must be elevated from the use of the tribe', we tribal members can only begin such an enterprise by speaking through the mouth of the tribe; the example frames our beginning; yet, to do the elevation under the auspices of the tribe is not to elevate at all. Consequently, the idea must be transformed from its status as an example (as tribal property) to a notion that exemplifies the history from which the tribe and its property are segregated.

One conventional way to describe the genre of which this book is an instance—a group of essays on different topics—is as a

11

B

collection. The problem that authors of a collection usually face, especially in their introductions, is to show what their separate papers have in common, to show some collecting procedure. Often, authors will try to show that although the papers appear to be about separate topics (and were written over a period of twenty years . . .) they really have one (or many) common theme(s). They are all about social structure or personality or meta-sociology.

What are our papers all about?

The topics could not have less in common. Any attempt to collect art, bias, snubs, motives, and evaluation by trying to imagine what they have in common would be as ludicrous as Wittgenstein's man who tries to find a rule for collecting all the tools in a toolbox. What all the tools in the toolbox have in common is that they are tools. What all our topics have in common is that they are topics. It is not that something becomes a topic for us by having something in common with something else but that we produce *anything* as a topic by dealing with it in terms of our version of inquiry. Anything can become a topic because anything can be inquired about. And the point of inquiring about anything—about bias, art, or travel—is not to describe bias, art, or travel, but to make reference to our commitment to inquiry. How we do analysis is shown by how we deal with these topics. It is pointless to look for our collection procedure in the topics we have chosen. Any topic could have been included in this book. We do not have a field, a special interest, or a point of view in the narrow substantive sense of these terms. Our field, our topic, is the nature of inquiry, i.e., the nature of that which makes possible all these papers. The papers are not collected in terms of what they are in themselves but in terms of how it was possible to produce them. Understanding how it is possible to collect them is understanding the method of analysis that collects them. The papers are attempts to show this method, by example.

The exemplary character of our speech explains a certain pervasive and, for some, puzzling feature of all our materials: we have no respect for members' usage. In every chapter, we (try to) do violence to members' conceptions of whatever phenomenon we are analysing: members claim bias is a trouble but we see it as an affirmation of positivism; members see snubs as a denial of recognition but we see them as a refusal to do analysis; members say motives cannot be analysed sociologically and we say they can; members explain their evaluations with reasons but we say that reasons explain only in the most superficial sense; members try to criticise art and relate it to its author but we say that these are impossible activities.

The usual understanding of violations of usage is that they are attempts to improve, make perfect, correct, or to remedy natural language. Such an enterprise has been shown to be misguided for reasons we have already indicated. We violate usage for a different reason. That we violate usage is a way of showing the difference between analysis and membership.[2] If we did not violate usage, if we were constrained by respect for members' conceptions of our topic, we would be exemplifying not analysis but membership. Our violations of usage are only puzzling to alters who deny the exemplary character of our speech. Only when speech is conceived of as other than example (as perfect) is it possible to respect usage and yet to theorise. The simple reason for this is that exemplary speech which respects usage is merely members' speech. From our perspective there can be no perfect speech if by that is meant it can unequivocally establish consensual agreement. Consequently, theorists who respect usage are acting under the auspices of the expectation of perfect speech, and are not theorists at all but rather members.

Behind this last point is our conception that any speech (and not just ours) can be conceived to exemplify the auspices which make it possible. This is to say that it is not, as some might have it, that other theorists talk about the world while we only talk about ourselves. Instead all analysis—functionalism, critical sociology, survey research—is about itself in that it displays nothing but its own version of authoritative inquiry. Analysis serves to produce its own example of itself. This is the essential activity of all modern sociology, whether functional, critical, or ethnomethodological. We try in the papers that follow to put you in touch with the essence of this activity.

So far we have alerted you to the importance of collaboration as a way of generating, exemplifying, and preserving in speech the

[2] By member we mean one who participates in everyday life as described on pp. 10–11.

organisation of an analytic commitment. In this collection four of us sought to concretise the idea of collaboration by working together: yet this might deflect you from grasping our essential point that analysis is a collaboration that occurs within the language of the speaker. Thus, while we produced this collection by transforming our collaboration into the kind of conversation that is interaction, our primordial notion of collaboration makes reference to the conversation within language and in this sense the 'relation' between ego and alter can be re-presented as the dialectical engagement between the speaker and his tradition which is exemplified in his course of thought. At this point we shall invigorate our discussion of dialectic without the terminological constraints that attend conventional speech in social science.

The thinking that is Rational is the dialectically evolving movement within language that is only exemplified in speech and which preserves the tension and irregularity of this movement. Inter-action between persons is not necessary for this, nor is every inter-action between persons necessarily such movement. For example, if we read Plato not as a biographer of Socrates and not as a reporter of those innumerable engagements between Socrates and his interlocutors, we could see him as making reference to the theoretical life, to the soul of an ideal theorist. As a course of action the soul (making reference to language) re-presents an ideal course of thinking as a movement from involvement in what appears to an engagement in the grounds of speech.

In the earlier dialogues the interlocutors appear as 'persons', independent of Socrates, who fail to exemplify such a course of action in contrast to the theorist-as-hero who does. But if we conceive of each interlocutor as an alter-ego, or objection, which the theorist ought to generate for himself, every dialogue becomes the trace of an essentially inward exchange reflected in the theorist's struggle to speak faithfully by freeing himself from the dispersed mouthings of his self-centred interests and the Desire for truthful speaking. The theorist collaborates with the Gods by seeking to affirm his loyalty through a kind of speech which wrests from concealment that which his self-interest hides. The interlocutors personify the theorist's own self-interest, and the conversation within the soul that Plato speaks of as theorising is a contest between self-interest and truth that

14

marks the theorist apart because of all men he knows the difference. Dialectic thought does not need a contest between persons. In fact it is easy to imagine that such a situation would draw us away from language in the interests of our own speech.

Thoughtful speech is speech which ought to preserve in its accomplishment a sense of this contest, a sense of its achievement. Because thoughtful speaking is speaking which shows that it listens to the Gods rather than to self, speaking can only appear as thoughtful by showing the dialectical achievement of such a hearing. Thoughtful speaking is essentially historical and the history it shows is the tension of a contest—a contest between origin and achievement—rather than the linearity of a method.

Speech is analytic when it is consistent with itself. For us this means: since the very accomplishment of speech makes reference to its achieved character, speech which is true to itself makes reference to the fact (and mystery) of its grounds. Speech which is truthful to itself is not self-centred because it is faithful to the analytic conception of speech as grounded speech and this very idea points beyond speech to that which causes all things to endure, to persist, and to be. Speech which is true to itself is speech which re-cognises that it is not self-sufficient, that it is not first but derivative. True speech recognises the difference between time and eternity.

Concrete speech ignores its achieved character, violates itself and conceives of itself as first. When concrete speech attempts to locate its grounds it points to 'external' nature, to 'internal' mind(s), to the self-organising activity of speech itself, or to past events under the delusion that such 'sources' are external to speech. These sources are presumed to be the origins of speech, and so the delusion consists in thinking that origin is that part of speech which is self-organising. It is as if bias, say, could originate in speech which defines and delimits bias. Concrete speech ignores the fact of its togetherness with these so-called sources, as different disclosures of speech itself, and thus conceals from itself its dependency upon that which is beyond it. In Plato's language concrete speech (at its best) formulates its grounds as ideas, forgetting that the ground of speech is that which surpasses idea.

When concrete speech does not see analytic speaking as narcissistic or capricious it will often see it as nihilistic, because the unformulability of grounds *seems* to mean that the object of analysis is nothing (is silent). But there is a difference between nothing and no-thing, for while it is true that the so-called object of analysis is no-thing in the sense that it is not a thing, it is not true that this object is nothing. We must note that the *what* (quiddity) of ground is not formulable, or characterisable, because grounds are not a determinant thing; the 'that' of ground is enunciated or announced in every intelligible speech. Being does not show itself in itself but announces itself through phenomena which show themselves. The analyst is one who is committed to this re-cognition and who seeks to speak under its auspices.

The idea of theorising makes necessary a distinction between the concrete and the analytic. In so far and whenever a theorist fails to formulate a distinction between the concrete and analytic—between concrete and analytic speech—he loses his ability to account for his own activity: for theorising. Without a distinction between the concrete and the analytic we necessarily formulate theorising as a reproduction or reporting of what appears. Any attempt to conceive of theorising as more than such imitation must make reference to the activity of speaking as that which seeks to go beyond appearance. For theory to be possible there must be a difference and also a relationship between how things appear and the way they are: a difference if theorising is to be anything more than reportage; a relationship if theorising is to be anything more than sheer self-display. Thus it would not be correct to believe that the concrete–analytic distinction is capricious, because it is a necessary condition of our existence. Although we cannot 'see it', i.e., observe it, we know it is there. In the language of Socrates we 'divine' the distinction in the sense that though we cannot know it directly in the way we can know a thing, we know it as a condition of our possibility, it is our ground, it is not nothing. Therefore the distinction is necessary for our own activity of theorising because to deny the distinction would be to affirm ourselves as mere imitators or reporters of appearance. To admit the distinction, on the other hand, is to use it as a way of accounting for our theorising which itself cannot be provided for simply by reference to the organised appearances of everyday life.

The social scientist's interest in ideas is an interest in the application of thought to things. Social scientists are interested in how things control thought (empiricism), how thoughts are themselves accomplished as things (rationalism); reflexive social science is interested in how thinking is constituted as a product—as the kind of thing which can be oriented to in standard, univocal ways (philosophy of science), or in how thinking is 'caused' by 'things' like society, groups, classes, and world views (so-called radicalism). We, on the other hand, are not interested in terminating our analysis with descriptions of things, or in using our ability to speak about things in an orderly way as criteria of successful analysis; nor are we interested in reporting or characterising the evolution and genesis of things as they are produced or as they appear. Our concern with such productions is reflected in our seeing them as occasions for renewing our own collaboration called analysis, because it is on such occasions that we become engaged with the question of possibility itself. This interest in possibility as reflected in each of the following papers is our concern with the difference between Being and nothing (between language and silence).

In this sense we would say that our analyses show their rational character in so far as our speaking constitutes itself as a dialectical engagement with the grounds of speech itself. Concrete speech, which treats itself as secure, contradicts itself because the very occurrence of intelligible speech makes reference to its achievement (and speech which treats itself as secure claims that it is first, natural, and has no history). Intelligible speeches then present occasions for resolving contradictions. For analysis, the contradiction which constitutes a problem resides in the form of a claim to be the whole, the very making of which denies the claim. This is to say that what appears as a disclosure of something else claims to be self-sufficient, unconditioned, and first; yet if that which appears were self-sufficient or first, to speak about it would be banal. Analysis resolves the problem by showing through the particular speech the problem itself. The truth which the speech covers over is that speech appears as a participant or subject and not as ruler. Thus, to say that analysis raises problems rather than solves them is to say that analysis brings to light the contradiction which every speech re-presents by treating the speech as an appearance of that which grounds it. The problem for analysis is always the difference, and to resolve the problem is not equivalent to eliminating the difference—the success of the solution to a problem does not reside in its elimination of a difference—but in making the difference between speech and language transparent.

Whether in the form of ordinary examples or in the works of men, problems appear as occasions to resolve contradictions. The contradiction is between the received conventional reading of the work or example and the understanding which that reading covers over. Analysis is the attempt to make this contradiction transparent by removing the cover from that which is covered-over. The contradiction which the treatment of every problem brings to light discloses in a particular form the omnipresent and eternal difference between being and Being as that between speech and language. Though examples and works are spoken about in such a way as to preserve their apparent differences as disclosures, they are also treated as similar with respect to the power of Being of which they are icons. Examples are then the same (displays of the original difference between Being and being) and different (intelligibly distinct displays).

If the contradiction is between the claim to truthfulness of the apparent, i.e., the claim to be first, and the grounds of this claim which is covered-over, the contradiction (as a problem) is resolved by speaking in such a way as to make reference to the Desire to uncover the covered-over. The concretisation of this desire in speech occurs as speaking seeks to address grounds of speech by organising itself as a display of the difference between achievement and ground, between speech and language. The movement of writing seeks to re-enact the movement of being from Being and since *that* difference cannot be spoken, writing seeks to show it by re-creating a difference and then by resolving it on any occasion (in any example). Analysis begins by fabricating the unity which is organised around conventional opinion as a topical resource (a unity that idealises and typifies some conventional truth, some secure understanding such as bias or snubs) and proceeds to dissolve this unity by showing how the unity participates in understandings which it leaves unsaid. Finally this difference is 'resolved' when it is shown to be a disclosure of the original difference between being and Being and *that* difference acquires its status as original precisely because it symbolises the firstness and comprehensiveness of the whole. Analysis resolves the difference not by creating a concrete unity but by showing the difference as original and irreducible; analysis 'resolves' differences (which it it-self creates) by using every occasion to re-create the difference in a concrete topic; analysis resolves problems by making problems transparent. It is in this sense that analysis succeeds when it reminds; to do analytic writing is to convince one-self that one has reminded. The rationality of analysis consists not in giving compelling concrete reasons to an other person but in doing an intelligible kind of reminding in writing, i.e., to do the kind of writing which shows itself as intelligible reminding.

The creative character of analysis is its re-creation of the difference, but this is more than virtuosity since the creation makes reference, in *its* achievement, to the original difference which enables creativity and makes it possible. The re-creation which is analysis is a way of making reference to the original creation as the possibility of any creation.

Analytic writing is then prepared as a display of the tension involved in the difference. The action of thinking as it first collects and then disperses in an effort to re-collect the covered-over is what we orient to in writing; writing seeks to evoke a sense of the achievement of the covered-over; writing seeks to preserve a 'sense' of this tension without degenerating into surrealism. Such dialectical or analytic writing attempts to preserve in its very organisation the Socratic methods of the *aporia* (the disillusion of the security of the hypothesis by transforming it into pathlessness), the *elenchus* (the sense of Socratic irony which in attempting to differentiate between chatter and meaning treats words as icons of language), and *anamnesis* (the effort to reconstruct and reorganise resonances which have become alienated from the idea). The Socratic dialogue is then preserved in speech as a movement which evokes the tension and irregularity of the contest within the soul idealised as true thinking.

Each of the papers that follow uses the topic named in the title in order to re-create the difference between being and Being in a Rational way. Each re-creation seeks to preserve the tension that symbolises this difference. We *use* the idea(s) of bias, snubs, travel, etc., to evoke an intelligible display of the difference between the grounds and products of speaking: the

19

intelligible display shows the achieved character of speech in the example-at-hand, i.e., the essentially grounded character of speech about snub shows the essentially grounded character of speech. In each case then, our speech seeks to be faithful to this re-cognition in the only possible way, by re-affirming it. We accomplish such affirmation by repudiating on each occasion the concrete everyday impulse to treat our own speech as a thing and we succeed to the extent our speech displays its essential source in no-thing. To re-create this dialectic is to reassert the resonant character of language by continuously and seriously engaging the idea as a display of that which grounds it.

That we have succeeded is testified to by reactions to this introduction and to our teaching. Objections to our speech have been made on the principle that it does not treat speech as a thing, and regardless of the variety of responses to our work they all participate in a similar understanding: to treat speech as no-thing is to be unresponsive to the requirements of some communal law. Complaints about data, test, validation, meaning and evidence are basically symptoms of this uneasiness because each of these complaints draws upon very particular communal disclosures of data, test, validation, meaning, and evidence which cover over the origins of such speech. We take these objections as a good sign if they represent having been put in touch with language. This book seeks to treat that something which is intelligible as speech (its intelligibility rests upon our ability to discriminate it from silence) as something that is not a thing. Each paper then constitutes a particular preparation of our own speech to show this; each paper exemplifies the speaking that is analytic.

2 MOTIVE

Our intention is to explicate the sociological status of motives. We shall address this issue by describing how ordinary actors employ 'motive' as a practical method for organising their everyday environments. Since motive is used by ordinary societal members to manage their orderly routines, our explication will be a formulation of the ways in which members' practices are grounded in their knowledge. We shall suggest that all sociological conceptions require some version of the common-sense member (of his practical knowledge); and we shall depict motive as one common-sense device for ascribing social membership, since motives are used by members to link particular concrete activities to generally available social rules. Motive, then, is one collective procedure for accomplishing social interaction, and for sorting out the various possibilities for social treatment by linking specific act and social rules in such a way as to generate the constellation of social actions that observers call 'persons', 'members' and 'membership'.

Readers of an earlier draft commented upon the absence of

any mention of ethnomethodology as strange. Unfortunately there is no adequate description of ethnomethodology in the literature. So, for example, Denzin's paper[1] is hopeless not merely because of his misunderstandings, but also because of his inadequately concrete conception of analysis; e.g., in superficially focusing upon the surface features of the approach— the concern with 'meaning', with the 'actor's point of view', etc.—he loses sight of the analytic character of ethnomethodology and of analysis in general.

Wilson, on the other hand, may understand ethnomethodology but not what to do about it.[2] If ethnomethodology obviates literal description, then suggesting that we be 'more explicit and self-conscious' is regressive if not vacuous—it is only to ask that we improve on the same literal procedures. As to the contrast between this paper and ethnomethodology, we must first record the great influence of the writings of Garfinkel, though this influence has not worked itself out in our thinking in the ways it has in his students.[3] Ethnomethodology, as it is practised by these students, not only fails to supply our programme with its rationale but denies this rationale at critical analytic points. Ethnomethodology seeks to 'rigorously describe' ordinary usage, and despite its significant transformation of standards for conceiving of and describing such usage, it still conducts its inquiries under the auspices of a concrete, positivistic conception of adequacy. Ethnomethodology conceives of such descriptions of usage as analytic 'solutions' to their tasks, whereas our interest is in the production of the idea which makes any conception of relevant usage itself possible. Whereas ethnomethodology uses the ordinary world 'seriously' (they hope to solve analytic problems by doing naturalistic science on this world), we treat the everyday world as a proximate occasion for initiating inquiry and not as a 'fact' to be reproduced. In our respective attitudes toward ordinary language and the everyday world, we have about as

[1] Norman Denzin, 'Symbolic interactivism and ethnomethodology: a proposed synthesis', *American Sociological Review*, 34, December, 1969, pp. 922–34.

[2] T. P. Wilson, 'Conceptions of interaction and forms of sociological explanation', *American Sociological Review*, 35, Aug., 1970, pp. 697–710.

[3] Harold Garfinkel, *Studies in Ethnomethodology*, New York: Prentice-Hall, 1967.

much in common with ethnomethodology as Heidegger shares with Austin. Finally, ethnomethodologists would regard our task in this paper as a stipulative exercise in legislating the use of a 'concept', while we would treat such an objection as a failure of analytic nerve, as the typical positivist gambit (which goes back at least as far as Protagoras) of refusing to exercise analytic authority, despite the fact that such authority grounds their entire enterprise with its intelligibility. Some of these issues are taken up in detail later.

THE SOCIOLOGICAL POSSIBILITY OF MOTIVE

Social scientists tend to conceive of motives as private and internal characteristics of persons which impinge upon and coerce these persons into various behaviours. In this view, motives are seen simultaneously (1) as 'causal' antecedent variables (antecedent to the event of interest), and (2) as characteristic 'states' of persons engaging in the behaviour. We maintain that these senses of motive are inadequate because they issue from a common misconception of motive, namely that motives are concrete, private and interior 'mainsprings' that reside in people, rather than public and observable courses of action.

This misconception leads to the contention that motives are only peripheral to the classic tradition of, say, Marx or Durkheim—that human motivation plays the role of unstated premises and is properly disregarded for analytic purposes (the ecological argument), or requires explication only in order to account for more of the variance (the social psychological argument of Homans, and Inkeles).[4] [5] We contend, instead, that motive plays a central role in such traditions, a role we can recognise if we grasp its analytic status rather than its concrete character.

If sociologists have sought to understand and formulate descriptions of social action, and if the analytic status of social action resides in its character as behaviour which is normatively

[4] George C. Homans, 'Bringing men back in', *American Sociological Review*, 29, December, 1964, pp. 809–18.

[5] Alex Inkeles, 'Personality and social structure', in R. Merton, L. Broom, and L. Cottrell, eds, *Sociology Today*, New York: Basic Books, 1959, pp. 249–76.

oriented to the very same environment it constitutes, then motive can function as an observer's rule for deciding the normatively ordered character of behaviour. That is, motive is a public method for deciding upon the (sociological) existence of action. In this usage, motive is an observer's rule of relevance in that it represents a sociologist's decision (his election) as to how items of concrete behaviour are to be reformulated as instances of social action.

For example, the sociological import of economic determinism in Marx is not the impersonal effects of brute facts upon an organism, but rather his formulation of a meaningful environment constructed by and seen from the perspective of a typical actor. To say 'economic determinism exists' is to decide to formulate actors as oriented to selected particular features of their socially organised environments in such a way as to enable this orientation (now called 'the economy') to produce their routine actions. To describe economic determinism is then to assign a rule of relevance to actors which serves the purpose of explicating social structure by reference to their grounds of action (the economy) as a set of sociologically intelligible events of social structure (economic determinism).

The classic roster of terms used by sociologists—social class, community, religion, suicide, bureaucracy, conflict, and the like—all require in their various ways this sort of conception. Motive then, serves as a theorist's election that some rule is relevant for explicating the character of some event as an instance of action. Motive is not in this regard a thing in the world but a way of conceiving social action.

In a more precisely sociological sense, it is observers who introduce a topic into behaviour, whether motives or any other. Thus, to say that 'social class exists', or that some group is high on need achievement, is for an observer to decide that some collection of persons is oriented to their status as a collective actor and is to be conceived as acting under the auspices of such an orientation. When an observer asserts that the American workers constitute a social class, he is deciding that the collection conceivable as American workers presently show in their behaviour their status as a collective actor, the identity of which the observer provides on the basis of their relation to the instruments of production.

This is also the sense in which Weber's *Theory of Social and*

Economic Organization—particularly the sections in which he depicts types of social relationships—can be read in a fundamental way as a set of methods for conceiving of motives. Each relationship is a different method for formulating actors as acting under the auspices of relevances to which they are methodically and selectively oriented.[6]

The upshot of all this—that motives function as observers' rules of relevance—is that though motives might be described as personal properties or characteristics of persons, they acquire their analytic force as observers' rules for depicting grounds of conduct. Thus, conventional notions of motives as concealed premises, or as peripherals that increase variance, are incorrect in the fundamental sense that it is in the *observer's* ascription of such rules, and not in the state-of-affairs the ascriptions recommend, that the analytic status of motives resides. Motives are a way for an observer to assign relevance to behaviour in order that it may be recognised as another instance of normatively ordered action.

It should now be clear why motives cannot be private and internal; if motives are sociologically depicted in the ascription of rules, the ascription of rules itself requires (presupposes) the use of a language that is public and observable. Even when we speak of 'hidden' motives, we are of course engaged in fully intelligible and observable courses of treatment—some public criterion enables us to grasp the topic. So-called hidden motives, slips, and the like are observable states of affairs which can be discussed in sensible and concerted ways. To treat motives as private is to confuse the state of affairs which motives report with the analytic status of the term, which is supplied by the public and by generally available rules that make motive reports socially possible and observable modes of social action.

There may be a concrete psychological state-of-affairs that corresponds to a motive report. We do not address this and so are not trying to run psychologists out of business. Our purpose, again, is to describe analytically the social organisation of motive ascriptions as courses of social action.

[6] Max Weber, *The Theory of Social and Economic Organization*, trans. Talcott Parsons, New York: Free Press, 1964.

GRAMMATICAL AND FACTUAL PERSPECTIVES IN THE FORMULATION OF MOTIVE

We have said that motive is a term regularly employed by actors to accomplish their routine affairs. When practical actors are 'doing motives', they are engaged in formulating themselves and their environments, in constructing and treating with their common-sense courses of action. To say 'He had the jealous motive to murder her' is to do no more or less than lay out and characterise an environment in such a way as to report on a social state of affairs, to make some behaviour possible, to limit the use of other behavioural possibilities, and so forth. The sociological status of the idea rests on whatever must be known in order to produce motive-talk as a recognisable or observable course of action. To provide a motive, then, is to formulate a situation in such a way as to ascribe a motive to an actor as part of his common-sense knowledge, a motive to which he was oriented in producing the action. Thus, to give a motive is not to locate a cause of the action, but is for some observer to assert how a behaviour is socially intelligible by ascribing a socially available actor's orientation. (This is perhaps what some sociologists intend when they invoke phrases like 'actor's point of view', 'what it means to the actor', and 'significant symbol'.) Questions of orientation do not require factual solutions (they are not either true or false), but rather, grammatical solutions. To talk motives is to talk grammar.

At the same time, however, social psychologists have used motive as a technical term designed to unravel the causal patterning of a sequence of actions, e.g., need achievement as an antecedent of economic development.[7] One problem with such technical usage is that it does not reformulate motive

---

[7] J. W. Atkinson, ed., *Motives in Fantasy, Action, and Society*, Princeton: D. Van Nostrand, 1958; R. B. Cattell, *Personality and Motivation Structure and Measurement*, New York: World Book Co., 1957; Gardner Lindzey, *The Assessment of Human Motives*, New York: Rinehart, 1958, pp. 3–33; D. C. McClelland, J. W. Atkinson, and R. A. Clark, *The Achievement Motive*, New York: Appleton-Century-Crofts, 1953; Neil Smelser and William T. Smelser, 'Introduction', in Smelser and Smelser, eds, *Personality and Social Systems*, New York: Wiley, 1963; Robert W. White, 'Ego and reality in psychoanalytic theory', *Psychological Issues*, 3, 1963, pp. 71–141.

from the perspective of a practical member; i.e., it ignores motive as a social course of action, and so it fails to provide for the relevance of motive as an activity engaged in by practical members.

Technical versions, which causally locate motives in neural circuits, libidinal arrests and the like, reformulate what is essentially a member's device without respect for those relevances and interests of the member which generate the behaviours of interest to the technician. Whatever the efficacy of neural paths, they have no social relevance except as they can be understood to be employed by the members.

This is not a new criticism and has been stated most articulately by the British ordinary language philosophers.[8]

To treat motive as a cause, as in 'What was his motive for suicide?' is to commit one version of the fallacy which Austin[9] and others have discussed in detail: the fallacy of presuming that suicide is an act which somehow describes some antecedent state of mind which preceded or caused it. On the contrary, to recognise the act of suicide as an intelligible event-of-conduct is to assign to that behaviour its identity as social action, in this case by formulating a motive. Thus, motive is a rule which depicts the social character of the act itself. It is not that his suicide reports some antecedent depression, or that murdering his wife reports his jealousy, or that leaving the party reports upon his boredom. Rather, the character of the suicide, the murder, the departure are identified through the clarification of unstated circumstances which make these actions socially recognisable as suicide, murder and departure. To say 'I want a motive for the murdered wife' is not to say that I want merely his antecedent state of mind which the wife's murder follows, but is instead to explicate the situation (the context, knowledge, conditions) which makes the event socially possible (a recognisable murder).

The best criticism of the causal account of motive is to be found in Melden's *Free Action*,[10] in which he demonstrates that since any conception of a cause presupposes a description of the

[8] R. S. Peters, *The Concept of Motivation*, London: Routledge & Kegan Paul, 1958; J. L. Austin, *How To Do Things with Words*, New York: Oxford University Press, 1965.

[9] Austin, op. cit.

[10] A. I. Melden, *Free Action*, London: Routledge & Kegan Paul, 1961.

27

C

very action for which the cause is identified, these accounts violate the necessary assumption of the analytic independence of cause and effect in the Humean model of causality. That is, some thing cannot be cited as a cause of an event if this 'something' is involved (presupposed) in the very description of the event; analyses of motive accounts show that whatever is cited as a motive serves to characterise more fully and completely the event for which it is formulated, and cannot then be treated as independent of the event. Melden says: 'this explanation does not refer to a present moment, sliced off from what has gone before and what will follow, but to the present action as an incident in the total proceedings.'[11]

We have not seen successful demonstrations of objections to this position in the philosophical literature, for those who claim that motives *can* be causes, or that motives *do* explain, usually accomplish this by changing the sense of 'cause' and by treating 'explanation' concretely rather than analytically. Of course, motives *can* be causes if one uses cause in a different sense; our notion is that any different sense makes 'cause' a constituent feature of the action (i.e., a presupposed element of the action), and hence, not a 'cause' in the ordinary sense at all. But, one is free to do this. Second, motives do explain, but by providing a way to see 'cause' as an intelligible link, not by citing a cause.

This is why it is elliptical to assert that motive describes only and simply a state of mind, when instead it serves to demand an explication of the circumstances which confer upon this putative state of mind its reasonableness as an account. Because such an explication amounts to a theory or formulation, it would be more correct to say that the quest for a motive (why did he kill her?) is a request for a theory.

MOTIVE AS SURFACE STRUCTURE

We have sought to show that motive acquires its analytic character as a public (methodic) product rather than as a private 'state', and that it is to be understood grammatically (as part of the meaning of an action) rather than as a factual report on some contingent, antecedent event. However, we now want to show how the analytic sense of motive is not located

[11] Ibid., pp. 98–9.

through a report of usage, but rather by formulating the conditions of knowledge which make such usage possible.

One option to the technical causal idea is thought to be a conception of motives as members' purposes, reasons, justifications and accounts.[12] In this tradition, the actor is used by the observer as a research informant, whose report acquires analytic status because the actor is thought to be a privileged and exclusive source on questions of his motive.

The paradigmatic procedure here is to ask the actor, 'Why . . . ?' and expect him to cite a reason, goal, or intention, e.g., 'Why did you leave the party?'; 'Because I was bored'; 'In order to make my appointment'; etc. In some cases we take these reasons and call them symbols and meanings, but that sort of substitution does not really tell us much about the methodical ways in which such statements are generated to begin with—how, for example, the actor is constrained to cite a reason at all; how it takes the form it does (giving a reason instead of, say, telling a joke); how it comes to be acceptable to the hearer is that it *is* an answer. In other words, its status as a common-sense practical device, as opposed to mere idiosyncratic noise or gesture or cue, remains unstated. (We are not making a sampling argument here. Even when an unanalysed event occurs repeatedly, it remains only a regularity. Lacking analysis, we would still be without an understanding or description of it, regardless of the times and places it had been counted.) The methodic social and hence sociological feature of motive lies not in the concrete, substantive reason an actor would give for his behaviour, but in the organised and sanctionable conditions that would regularly produce the giving of a reason by a competent member in the first place. The reason given is no more than the surface expression of some underlying rule(s) that the former requires in order to be understood.[13]

[12] H. W. Gerth and C. W. Mills, *Character and Social Structure*, New York: Harcourt Brace and Co., 1953; Alfred Schutz, *Collected Papers*, Vol. I, The Hague: Martinus Nijhoff, 1962; Marvin B. Scott and Sanford Lyman, 'Accounts', *American Sociological Review*, 33, February, 1968, pp. 46–62; D. S. Shwayder, *The Stratification of Behaviour*, London: Routledge & Kegan Paul, 1965: New York: Humanities Press, 1966.

[13] Noam Chomsky, *Aspects of the Theory of Syntax*, Cambridge, Mass.: M.I.T. Press, 1965.

The surface performance which is displayed in the use of motive might be that of offering a reason, goal, or intention, but to provide an account of motive in these terms is to ignore the deep structure which makes the surface display possible at all. As we shall investigate, motivec aquires its analytic status by virtue of the fact that it requires for its use certain deep structures for conceiving of 'person', 'member', 'responsibility', 'biography', and the like; these deep structures are absolutely necessary for an ordinary member's competent and sensible employment of motive as a device, because they generate the variety of surface reasons he may cite in any particular case. It is through these deep conditions that an analytic conception of the ordinary sociological use of motive is provided.

It should be clear then, that the similarity which typical symbolic interaction accounts appear to achieve with our present formulation—through such phrases as 'vocabularies of motives' and the like—is misleading, for they treat concrete speech acts—such as giving reasons or justifications, or citing intentions—as providing an analytic explication of motive whereas we treat such usage as surface phenomena which are made possible by deeper conditions of knowledge. The concrete character of such versions of motive is conveyed in their practice of treating motive as the practical actor's expression of his knowledge, in contrast to the present suggestion that analytic status is supplied through some conception of an observer's method of constructing a practical actor (no matter what he is concretely taken to perform or say).

For example, Gerth and Mills cite Weber as we do, but interpret him as using motive as equivalent to 'an adequate reason for conduct'.[14] On the other hand, we are saying that this usage fails to capture the analytic character of motive as an *observer's decision to treat or reformulate* some behaviour as a reason, and that this is an entirely different matter. So too, they see motive as 'ascribed through talk',[15] and as a 'term' of the talk itself, whereas, in our view, speech is just a medium for the concrete expression of motive, but it is a set of prior and deeper conditions of knowledge which permit an observer to treat talk as intelligibly predicating motive. The symbolic interactionist finds it impossible to formulate a version of

[14] Gerth and Mills, op. cit., p. 116.
[15] Ibid., p. 114.

motive that is analytically distinct from conventional versions, because he still conceives of motive as a practical actor's concrete report of his state of mind: he only shifts his focus from the state-of-mind to the talk, by treating the talk as some sort of public indicator of the mind. Gerth and Mills show this quite explicitly when they eventually surrender to a concern for questions such as what the differences are between professed motives and 'real motives', and with the actor's degree of 'awareness' of his motives.[16] These are not the questions of those who have grasped the analytic character of motive.

Though more ingenious than most, Kenneth Burke is not exempt from these charges, for in his effort to locate the analytic parameters of motive, he confuses analytic and concrete conditions (i.e., the parameters of act, agent, agency, scene, and purpose). However, despite Burke's failure to explicate the grammar of motive, in more than a metaphoric sense, he performs a service by continually keeping before us the notion that the way in which priorities are allocated to these parameters is a function of a theoretic election (that it is observers who formulate motives), though we do not get a description of how such formulations are accomplished.[17]

We can now locate the major difficulty which unifies the various conventional accounts of motives, i.e., the conception which appears to unify the various sorts of troubles we have been discussing. These accounts pose the problem of motives as a factual rather than a grammatical one, which leads easily to the trap of treating motives as causes, as states-of-persons, and as concrete speech-acts such as reasons, accounts, and justifications. And these accounts treat motives as raising a concrete, factual question of 'why?' rather than as attempts to formulate the socially organised conditions under which such a question is sensible to those who raise it. Any strategy which equates the factual surface structure of motive talk with an analytic conception of motive cannot provide any more than a concrete and irrelevant record.

We are not prescribing how motive-talk should be accomplished; rather, we are stating that under any and all occasions of motive-talk in our society, to which we have reference, such

[16] Ibid., p. 119, p. 125.

[17] Kenneth Burke, *The Grammar of Motives*, New York: Prentice-Hall, 1945.

talk requires members to make certain assumptions about their environments. Furthermore, their talk shows that they make these assumptions. Again, whether members know these conditions, or can report them to us, is analytically irrelevant in the same sense that Chomsky's native speakers cannot concretely reproduce his theory even though they do show its correctness and provide for its formulability through their behaviour.

In sum, when we speak of motive, we have in mind neither the technical observer's notion of the causes of an action, nor the actor's report of why an action was done. We do not require either an explanation or reason for the action, but rather some description of the socially organised conditions which produce the practical and ordinary use of motive in the mundane affairs of societal members. To locate motive is thus not to 'find' anything but to describe the necessary and analytically prior understandings and conventions which *must* be employed in order for a member even to invoke motive as a method for making a social environment orderly and sensible.

THE DEEP STRUCTURE OF MOTIVE

A. MOTIVES ARE OBSERVERS' RULES

Motives acquire their analytic status as observers' rules. They are not forces or events in the world extraneous to an observer. Motives are sociologically possible only because some practical observer has methods and procedures—i.e., rules—for locating them as events in the world, not because that is where they really are. Because events cannot 'exist' sociologically except as courses of treatment, and because courses of treatment are not intelligible except through available social rule, motives cannot be located except by rule. Consequently, motives are accomplished exclusively through the use of such methods and procedures.

When a member says 'He had the jealous motive to . . .' we expect that the statement can be understood as a description of possible behaviour. Of course, there can be disagreement with the surface content of the statement—perhaps he did not have the jealous motive—but it nevertheless remains an intelligible

32

remark because it describes an understandable or socially possible motivated action. Others do not think every such statement literal nonsense. This is again to distinguish between concrete surface phenomena or causal properties (whether the object does or does not have the jealous motive) and the analytic deep structure that makes such phenomena possible (that an observer can talk intelligibly about jealous motive, whatever the factual status of his talk).

The point here is that there must be some rule—of language, interpretation, or culture—by which motive-talk takes life as a description.

Now to say that some rule is available is to remove the sociological habitat of motive from object (the person who had the jealous motive) to discourse about the object (how it is understood that a motive ascription has been made). This is to say, again, that the sociological import of motive resides in its procedural implications for the *treatment* of objects and not in the states of the objects themselves. Motive is a procedure.

This first feature brings motive into the full corpus of sociological ideas: rules must exist for such a procedure as motive to exist. They are socially organised treatments. Motive is not something an actor has—it is not a property of an actor. It is not something the sociologist decides that some person owns, in the sense that it is the 'thing' which he owns. Rather, motive is a member's method for deciding what alter owns. Thus, the sociologist does not search for motives in objects of talk and treatment, but in the talk and treatment itself.

Note, though, that the concrete talk—the speech act(s), the usage—does not provide the observer with the motive (as some versions of sociology might have one believe), but such analytic status is located in terms of the observer's decision as to what must be known in order to recognise in the talk, the analytic 'presence' of motive.

One socially organised condition for addressing the topic of motive, therefore, is the assumption of the availability or relevance of a motive ascription rule. The necessary availability of such a rule, or rules, can be seen by noting that motives are a common-sense class of events, in that to do (observe) motives is not to be exclusively doing (observing) something else (writing a play, sleeping). That motives are the topic in any case, as opposed to some other topic or no topic, requires that others understand they are the topic, which in turn requires that the socially available rule for introducing the class 'doing motives' be displayed in the behaviour of the introducer. As with any form of social behaviour, the members themselves conceive the doing of motives to be rule-guided. Thus, one kind of common-sense-sociological rule is the motive ascription rule, and the most elemental necessary feature of this deep rule is: there are rules for the ascription of motives.

B. MOTIVATED OBJECTS ARE THEORISERS

One rule for the ascription of motives therefore is that the observer-user knows there are motive-ascribing rules. A concomitant of this first rule is that the ascriber know (assume, presume) that the *object* knows there are motive-ascribing rules.

In order to be called motivated, the object of an ascription cannot be treated as if he were doing the behaviour haphazardly or coincidentally. He is, in other words, treated as if he has the capacity to 'know what he's doing'. Any object thought to be unable to know what it is doing cannot be treated as motivated, even though that object resembles a human organism, e.g., a brute or an infant. That ascribers know there are rules, requires that they impute this knowledge to the object. Otherwise, the ascriber's knowledge could not be conceived by him to be a practical guide to the object's behaviour, since the latter could not be deemed to be oriented.

(We should perhaps remind the reader here that the phrase 'knows there are rules' does not imply 'knows *the* rules'. All kinds of substantive mistakes and arguments over content and application may occur in the course of motive ascription without ever denying that there are rules. What the rules are, and that rules exist, are two quite different ideas, and correspond to our previous distinction between surface and deep structure, respectively. This same distinction carries through to 'knowing what he's doing'. We can be quite mistaken about what it is we are doing without being treated as if we *couldn't* know, e.g., as in therapy.)

Alter, as rule-guided, incorporates the fundamental sociological principle that generally available rules are the analytic equivalent of membership (community, group, pair, etc.). Rules make actors' methodicity and concert possible by transforming what would otherwise be nonsense into intelligible social behaviour. That alter can be conceived (by observing ego and sociologist) to be rule-guided encompasses the status of motives within general sociology: motive, as with any other sociological classification, refers to certain actions by rule-guided ascribers and objects. The ascriber is rule-guided in his characterisation of an object, while the object is (assumed to be) rule-guided in his behaviour, and thus assumed to 'know what he's doing'. Both ego and alter assume of one another that they are, or could be, doing motives. Each is a theoriser, in the sense that both must be looking to rules in order to carry off their activity as doing motives. For motive treatment to occur, as for any kind of membership treatment to occur, ego and alter must necessarily generate for one another their status as members oriented to rules. Here a set of concrete activities is so formulated that those activities become members through the application of a corpus of rules. This is a detailed way of saying they are members of a social relation.

Take, for example, the brute. There are things which can be said of such an organism, e.g., it is enraged, it is contented, it is sleeping, and so forth. These are characterisations, in that they depict some state of affairs, and rule-guided ascriptions at that. But they are not, and could not be, common-sense ascriptions of motives because the brute's behaviours are not thought to be displays by a rule-guided actor—the brute is thought not to be socially 'responsible'. He is thought not to be responsible in so far as his activity is, in Weber's terms, behaviour rather than action. Nor is the brute thought to be a bona fide member, and for the same reason: he cannot be a member because he cannot be said to know what he's doing through an orientation to member rules.

By 'rule-guided' we do not mean that actors are automata governed by abstract rules, that rules are clear and unchanging and automatically applied, or that it cannot be difficult, confusing, and vague for members to act like members. We do not mean that actors are rule-governed.[18] On the contrary, it is those who can behave but not act whom we conceive to be rule-governed automata, for they seem only to play out as mechan-

[18] Jonathan Bennett, *Rationality: An Essay Towards Analysis*, London: Routledge & Kegan Paul, 1964: New York: Humanities Press, 1964.

isms the untransformed universal needs and drives of every man. Universals remain constants for the brute, and they govern him in the sense that they are not given the differentiated and variable expression that we think of as motivated social action. Jealousy can be a motive precisely because it is not universal in husbands. Think of thirst as a motive here—what would it be like to enact the thirst drive in such a way as to have it said that 'he killed her because he was thirsty'? The distinction between rule-governed and rule-guided is comparable to the one between behaviour and action, and it is surely correct that the use of rules by members is an accomplishment in the hardiest sense of the term. We are only asserting that ego and alter must assume, however difficult, the application of substantive ascriptions, that *some* corpus of membership rules is being used in behavioural displays before they can be characterised by substantive motive schema. It is necessary that ascriber and object are assumed to be of a certain kind, namely theorisers.

We are not suggesting, either, that members always neatly agree on what is happening around them, or that the substance of rules is common to all interactants. Whether behaviour goes well or badly, whether it 'deviates' or 'conforms', is not an issue. We do not equate the deep notion of theoreticity with the substance of interaction. Theoreticity is the observed, rule-guided identification of the doing of anything at all, whether well or badly, whether deviant or conforming. (Even to be considered one or the other requires that some imputation of rule be used.)

Take the case of mental illness. If the person is conceived by members to be doing nothing in particular, to be merely a set of either random or universal behaviours, then no question of motive will ever arise (or will arise only once, to be dismissed by the finding of nonmembership). Only when being crazy can be seen as organised or rule-guided—again, as being a display of some membership—does the possibility of motivated mental patients occur.

To be theoretic is thus to be conceivable by some observer as methodically rule-guided, rather than haphazard in behaviour. To ascribe a motive, among other ascriptions, is of course to formulate the intelligible character of some behaviour. The warrant for motive ascription is that the object be theoretic, that his behaviour is capable of being formulated as action, just as it is the warrant for any common-sense facet of membership.

C. MOTIVES HAVE A GRAMMAR

A third organised condition of motive ascription is a grammar that locates for a potential or would-be ascriber those conditions in the world which give notice that an ascription is to be done. The grammar moves a motive rule into behaviour, from availability to ascription. It is a (collection of) rule(s) of use for the doing of an ascription. It depicts for the observer a procedure for actually ascribing available designations to a world populated by members. The grammar links a phenomenon in the world to the available corpus of designations.

This grammar of motives is used whenever an event is to be collected within a biography. We may think of the biography as a collection of 'owned experiences', in that actors conceive themselves as having particular pasts which routinely inform an observer about the possibilities for their behaviour; and we may think of events as some observer's definition of a situated environment of objects, specific to time and place. Motives are the social characterisations, generally available, the grammar which is used when biography and event are to be linked. The grammar produces for the ascriber a relation between some practical phenomenon and the common-sense biography with which that event now comes to be associated through the process of ascription. A common-sense biography is the observer's version of a set of owned experiences (husband), a set which comes into contact with, or is juxtaposed against, particular concrete (and hence socially problematic) phenomena in the world (dead wife). The grammar is the rule (connect the experience—husband—with the event—dead wife) that conjoins the two as an accomplishment of organised and concerted treatment (a jealous motive).

Imagine a hypothetical community where a murder is committed, and the husband of the victim is eventually identified as the killer. Initially, everyone could be suspect, and to 'look for the motive' is to address the links between the murder and various collections of owned experience in the community. The ways these experiences are joined with murdered wife methodically generate the motivated (or not) character of any link.

The idea of motive thus serves to formulate for members their interactions, in so far as they conceive interaction as

37

experiences framed in events. Actors are thought by observers to have biographies and to engage the world with them. The grammar produces the link between the two. Motives are resources for connecting an event with a biography, and they generate the event as a member of the class of experiences owned by a body (as depicted in common sense).

Similarly, motives depict for us how the event shows or displays a biography. In so far as the biography and the event can be seen to be membership, this is done through the ascription of motive. Otherwise—in the absence of such a grammar—observers would be unable to organise the current and flow of socially intelligible events, nor could they observe the products of biography; i.e., they could not see interaction as a course of history. They would be without a temporal method. Events could only be seen to be performed and disembodied, not enacted by some theoretic–nontheoretic incumbent of a situated social world. Motives thus characterise biographies enacting events, are specific to events, and distinctive of biographies. They are a grammar in that they methodically collect these disparate phenomena. And they are social in that they transform what would otherwise be fragmentary series of unconnected immediate events into generally intelligible social courses of behaviour. It is through motive as a culturally available designation that the observer recovers alter's membership out of observed temporal phenomena, because motives delineate the biographical auspices of acts in situations.

D. MOTIVES FORMULATE A TYPE OF PERSON

The grammar, then, includes some collection of owned experiences which can be allocated to the agent of the act, and some rule(s) for showing the related character of the event and the collection of experiences. Because there are alternative collections (of experience) available, the use of the grammar poses a selectional problem for its user in this sense; it has to include a search procedure for deciding the relevance of one biography (one collection) as compared to other possibilities. The search procedure is essentially the rule for showing the *possible* relevance of the biography for the event. Such a rule amounts to the formulation of a type-of-person.

Thus, when users formulate the biography called 'husband',

the relevance of which to the event 'murdered wife' is decided through a formulation of circumstances and characteristics such as jealousy, they are formulating the biography (husband) as the type of person whose jealousy could produce the event of murdered wife. In this way the grammar is a provision for explicating the link between the biography and the event and this explication is supplied by the formulation of a type of person.

The grammar of motives enables members regularly to address the fact that the relevance of biography to event is formulable through a rule which locates the owner of the biography as the type of person who would do the event. (While we separate these features of the grammar for analytic purposes, they are concretely indistinct. As one formulates a biography of owned experiences presumed to be relevant to the event, this presumption can already be informed by an unstated rule which has decided that relevance as the kind of person who would do the event.) Type of person, then, explicates the circumstances and understanding required to assert the relevance of any biography for the event. The heart of the grammar is thus its rule for formulating a type of person. It is in this sense that any observer's ascription of a motive serves to formulate for some activity, a person.

E. MOTIVES FORMULATE ACTORS' METHODS

If the application of the grammar is equivalent to the formulation of a type of person, what is required of such a formulation? Note that type of person is an identification of certain characteristics, traits, dispositions, and behaviours which make ownership of the biography relevant to the event. While the items on such a list (characteristics, traits, dispositions, behaviours) all tend to itemise concrete features of the person, they only acquire their analytic sociological interest as descriptions of possible ways of relating to the event, i.e., as potential courses of action. To formulate a type of person is to formulate a course of action on the grounds that no matter what one predicates substantively of persons to make their biographies relevant to the event, such relevance is only assigned on the assumption that the predicates predict a typical, possible course of action. Person, then, depicts a typical possible actor.

To say his motive in murdering his wife was his jealousy, is to explicate the circumstances which make him the type of jealous person who would (could) murder his wife—that murdering his wife is one possible method available to him for doing jealousy. In this way, the event is formulated as the agent's possible method for doing whatever the formulation of the motive requires as a course of action.

He killed himself because he was depressed, or he left the party because he was bored—both are observers' ways of saying that killing oneself is a method of doing depression, or that prematurely leaving the party is a way of doing boredom. This understanding is important because members regularly raise the question of motive and address it as a sensible topic only of those classes of events which are recognisable as possible products of actors' methods. Questions such as 'What was your motive in spilling the ink?' or 'What was your motive in speaking so softly?' come up in ordinary usage when something is fishy, *and* when it is sensible to ascribe to an actor some methodic display of intention or purpose.[19] To assign a motive is then necessarily to assume that the event exhibits possible methodicity.

As we have stated, at the deepest level such methodicity is addressed in the observer's conception of the event as showing the agent's character as a type of person—by the agent's being formulable as a possible method, as it were, to 'do' whatever type of person which he is formulated as. Perhaps, this is what Aristotle intended in the following: 'acts are called just and self-controlled when they are the kinds of acts which a just or self-controlled man would perform, but the just and self-controlled man is not he who performs these acts, but he who also performs them in the way just and self-controlled men do'.[20] The observer assumes, then, that the agent shows in the event (uses the event as) one possible method of identifying himself through his action as a particular type of person: that the murder of his wife identifies him as a jealous type of person, leaving the party as a bored person, and so forth.

When an observer formulates a member in this sense, he is

[19] J. L. Austin, 'Three ways of spilling ink', reprinted in J. H. Gill, ed., *Philosophy Today,* No. 1, New York: Macmillan, 1968.

[20] Aristotle, *Nicomachean Ethics*, Indianapolis: Bobbs-Merrill Co., 1962, p. 39.

stipulating that whosoever he is formulating has knowledge to act under the auspices of his (the observer's) formulation of a type of person. The formulation of a type of person (of one who has a motive) thus requires the observer to assume that the one so formulated is capable of 'showing' the type of person for which the observer's formulation provides. Therefore, when the observer formulates a motive, he is formulating a type of person and is required to assume that the one so formulated is a member in the deep sense of the term, i.e., as one who can generally be expected to know what he's doing in the possible circumstances where he might or could be doing it, circumstances which include those of motive ascription.

No matter what members conceive themselves to be doing when they ascribe motives, we say they are engaged in conceiving others (or self) to be doing whatever activities they do because they 'own' a particular collection of experiences which can be used as a normative order for creating sensible events. Those to whom motives are ascribed are thus formulated under the auspices of the following requirements: (1) That they treat such a collection of experiences as possible grounds of action in situations, (2) that other collections of experiences are possible alternative grounds of action, (3) that the activity which is done is the actor's way of showing, to the one who ascribes, the relevance of his own collection of experiences (of showing himself as a type of person), and (4) since every kind of showing as a type of person is a method of excluding other possible persons, that the actor as *this* type of person is selectively doing whatever he comes to (since according to his theoretic status in common, he could have come to something else). It is in these ways that regular motive ascriptions are regularly introduced in regular social intercourse; it is in these ways that motives formulate actors' methods.

In summary, we have attempted to depict the socially organised conditions which members tacitly accredit in their accomplishment of motive as a sensible and observable event. We have tried to demonstrate that motive can be sociological by showing that motive shares with all matters of sociological interest (class, bureaucracy, suicide, etc.) a status as a common-sense formulation. Motive depicts, for any observer, a course of social action.

Motive is a sociological procedure for describing how

organisms show themselves as persons. To gain an identity as a person requires that disparate activities and experience can be collected by actors under some typification, a process which makes the activities graspable for them through the formulation of alter's motivated identity. The condition of membership in common makes it possible for an observer to expect that alter, because he knows what he's doing and hence is responsible, will use common rules as a standard of orientation when he displays his biography in situations, thus knowledgeably revealing his type of person.

Given (the observer's imputation of) alter's capacity for knowing what he is revealing, together with his being a differentiable type of person, the observer can also warrantably conceive alter's future, and thus organise not just the current biography and event, but future links between the two as well. Motives are a procedure for organising an historic and regular interactional future.

Most fundamentally, then, whatever a motivated actor does will show his methods for affirming himself as a person. Being responsible and capable of displaying some other collection of owned experiences, the observer is permitted to note that he nevertheless did display the collection he displayed. For any member to ascribe a motive is thus to do no less than to generate a person. It is to formulate from situated performances a responsibly displayed and differentiated collection of experience.

While each of these public and rule-guided conditions must exist for motive ascription to occur sensibly, they can of course be accomplished in a variety of substantive ways which we have not discussed here. For example, that there is a grammar under which a motive ascription rule is invoked suggests that members regularly differentiate between activities which do and do not require the use of that grammar; i.e., there are some activities which needn't be organised according to motive criteria. In the same vein, there are undoubtedly a variety of methods in use by which members identify organisms as possible theoretic actors, e.g., the various ways it is decided that a child is enough of a member to be called a theoretical actor and so a potential object of motive ascription.

More centrally, one pervasive feature of social organisation concerns members' methods for tracking and formulating biographies from a universe of possibilities, and the various rules for deciding the relevance of particular biographies as particular types of persons. The bureaucratic method, for instance, is probably very different from the familial one. All these are categorisation problems which members regularly resolve, methodically producing the organisation of their everyday environment. To describe such particular solutions requires other studies, the possibility of which we can now begin to grasp. Being interactional and rule-guided—being a social method (just as bureaucracy, social class, or institutionalisation are methods)—confirms that the status of the deep structure of motive is sociological.

ADDENDUM

As we review this motive paper in terms of our current analytic interest reflected by the other studies in this volume, it is obsolescent in certain important respects. This is not to say we reject the paper, for it stands as an underdeveloped and inarticulate expression of the same commitment we now show. We honour the paper as re-presenting a developmental point and the following comments are intended only to discriminate our current interest in grounded speech from the same interest as it was shown in that paper.

We can note first that the paper on motives is really about sociology. The topic is the social and not motive at all; further we understand it now as a paper dealing with the problem of language and the question of how to achieve a relationship between speech and language. The failure to see this in the beginning led to our organisation of that paper as a substituting or correcting operation, as if we were proposing a rational speech about the word motive as an alternative to current motive usage. Let us specify these objections.

In that paper we exempt our own talk from the same consideration—as speech requiring some relation to language— by absorbing it under notions of rule, grammar etc. Rule, grammar, theoreticity, and other dimensions used in the paper are descriptive versions of auspices, whereas the question we might now ask is what kind of world would make motive talk intelligible and interesting? That question would require that we address our own interest in motive talk, that we address

D

the fact that we find such talk interesting. Because motive talk represents an occasion of collectability and not just motive, we should have accounted for our interest in collectability as producing the concern with motive talk. Given our interest in collectability, the primary concern is not the problem of motive but of collecting the relationship of speech to language and that interest was distorted in the paper because it was transformed into a focus upon 'motive', which is merely a member's way of talking about collectability (because motive becomes like ground or language for members). In the paper we only imitated ordinary members by explicating or attempting to preserve their sense of motive as ground, whereas what we should have been doing was using motive talk as an occasion for addressing the problem of collectability that actually makes reference to the relationship between words and language.

Motive is not a rational way to look at grounds because motives are causal. They are causal in that members attribute motive as a reason for a state of affairs. In the paper we show that members' attributions of cause are different from the very concrete attributions of psychologists, of ascriptions of states of affairs to people, etc., but nevertheless our explication limits itself to the sense that motives remain causes within the context of the theorising of members. In the paper we merely explicate and preserve the ordinary sense of theoretic interest, whereas we would now be controlled by an entirely different notion of origin than cause. In other words we preserve through explication the ordinary member's notion of origin, but our interest in origin as shown in the following papers and in the introduction is quite different.

In the paper we accepted members' versions of origin and we showed this acceptance by being constrained by the notion of rule, grammar, theoreticity, etc., rather than seeing these so-called parameters as themselves icons of a tradition.

Yet, our interest in origin is equivalent to a concern with the kind of world or tradition which could produce any collection as a possibility (whether theirs or ours). In the paper we talked about how a particular kind of collecting—motive—proceeds without taking up the idea of collecting itself and which would have led us to ask the following question: how is it possible to produce a causal world? Now we can see that a causal world is a world in which things that one is with are treated as essentially enigmatic; where there is a continual process of clarifying the things one is with by making reference to things outside of them (things that are before, after, or external). In this world—the causal world—one knows what one is with only by assimilating it to what is different from what one is with (which one knows in the same way) and therefore the enigma is this: that one never has time for what one is with, one is always moving away, showing no patience and refusing to linger, one is moving away from the things themselves to other external, before, and after things, in order to provide accounts through comparison, relationship, and the like. This version of the causal world is then quite the opposite of the classical world. In the causal world the inquirer treats himself as enigmatic, as requiring clarification through reference to what is outside of him, or before him, or behind him, as a set of rules. Consequently, the enigmatic character of this world appears in the fiat that speech is the important thing, and given one's disregard of language the world must be enigmatic because one tries to move outside of language; when this happens words become segregated from language and therefore become things; and so, in this world things become separated from language in the ultimate, inexorable, concrete segregation.

Our analysis of motive today would provide for the enigmatic world which would produce a concern with motive as an interesting problem. In that world for example, the analytic segregation of the grounds of clarity (language) from the search for clarity (method) creates a preoccupation with method in itself (in rule) as the Good. In that world the source of any ascription or attribution is only methodic, however, and in the absence of language it ignores (fails to recognise) the solution that is sought. Any interest in the actual success of collecting, or in the criterion that one is able to accomplish collecting, or in the artfulness of collecting, shows itself in the treatment of method and rule as the Good. This can be seen clearly in our own speech about motive which terminates in its formulation of parameters such as rule. In contrast, we are currently interested in grounds of clarity or language as they become disclosed through *any* method or speech, whereas these grounds themselves are not the end (as if a determinant solution) but the beginning which authorises the very problem of motive, or method, or whatever. Thus, our interest is not in a solution because the solution is not an end, only representing or showing the interest and commitment to language, and consequently the end is what is displayed in such a showing.

We seek in these comments to clarify how a contemporary treatment of motive would be brought up to date with the analytic interest we show in other papers. In this sense we include motive to represent the inarticulate and underdeveloped conception of analysis of earlier works in order to make available a clearer sense of our own analytic commitment now.

Note: This paper originally appeared in the *American Sociological Review*, 1971, and it has been reproduced here without changes except that explanatory footnotes in the original article have been incorporated in the text.

3 BIAS

I. INTRODUCTION

In the social sciences bias conveys the idea that something can go wrong with a description unless certain precautions are taken to eliminate it. Although it is a possibility, bias is not a normal and expectable practice—rather, normal and expectable practices are designed to (1) rid us of bias; (2) when that cannot be done, to state it and thus somehow reduce its effects; (3) permit us to recognise bias when we see it. In other words, bias is a trouble.

Our task here is to inspect the idea of bias as it is conceived by those who deal with it. What is bias, what grounds are invoked in charging bias, what are the rules and grammars for recognising the bias that these grounds generate? Through such an examination we hope to offer an example of a certain kind of sociological analysis, to make reference to *our* grounds for depicting the usage of bias as we do.

Thus, we want to understand bias as a feature of the socially organised environment of social scientific inquirers, i.e., as an

order to which they seek to comply. Our interest in how bias
is used is not an interest in characterising, codifying, or organising such usage: rather, we *use* such usage to make reference to
speech that protects its grounds from scrutiny and this example
then provides us with an occasion to exemplify speaking which
is engaged in grounds. Our very use of bias talk as an example
of protective speech is only possible because of our (contrasting)
commitment to an engagement with grounds. Thus, we do not
reject the idea of bias, we analyse it: we *do* reject the idea of a
commitment to protect the auspices of speaking, because that
kind of commitment rejects dialectic. Since we use bias in this
study as an example of protective speech, we necessarily reject
this usage, but it is obvious that we accept the (analytic) idea
of bias in so far as we use it as an occasion to show our conception of analysis.

II. BIAS AS A THING TO BE ELIMINATED

Bias is conceived in the social sciences to be a troublesome thing.
Not simply troublesome, but a troublesome *thing*. In this
respect it has its own special properties, these properties can
actually exist, and so when these properties exist bias exists.
Persons who are interested in bias are similar to the believers
whom Socrates discriminated from true philosophers:[1] like the
pursuit of beautiful things, the concern with bias is a concern
with whether a 'thing' (speech treated as a thing) *appears*
biased or reliable. Because a thing which appears biased can
also appear unbiased, the 'object' for the believer is not the
Real but something which changes and becomes. Just as the
beautiful thing is grounded in the idea of beauty-as-beauty, so
the imputation of bias to a speech is grounded in the idea of
bias.

To ask how bias could be seen as a trouble in the first place
begins to address the idea; the context of understandings which
provide for the conception of bias as a deformity which appears
in speech makes reference to a notion of adequate speech which
this very conception protects. It is this conception which we
desire to bring to light; we want to make the distinction between

[1] Those who interest themselves in beautiful things rather than the
idea of beauty itself.

whether or not the speech is biased and how bias is biased (how the use of bias is faithful to our analytic notion of bias). The conception we are examining is applied to speeches as if bias is a resource whose use is simply a matter of application to concrete things in the world and it treats the problem of the possibility of bias as a concrete problem of applying the universal to the particular. In contrast, we want to use the myriad applications of bias to unearth the idea that constrains and to make this constraint itself transparent in terms of whether or not it shows a dialectical engagement with itself (with its history and grounds).

Rather than accepting that bias exists in the way it is thought to exist, we want to ask how this troublesome character of bias is intelligible by asking what idea generates the possibility of such a view of bias in the first place. A central question will be: what form of life can we formulate such that it generates for social scientists their organisation of intelligible and concerted speech about bias? Further, how do the resonances of bias alert us to that which social scientific use shares with all use? Finally how does this examination itself generate as a possibility the image of a dialectical engagement in the question of grounds, and how does such an image make reference to our conception of analysis?

The very idea of eliminating bias is degenerate because it reminds us that the received use of the notion treats bias as the way in which a thing can *appear*. That bias can be eliminated means that bias is an appearance, because the idea of elimination recommends the contingent character of that which shows itself as bias. Bias is like a social problem—here today and gone tomorrow—and the reformulation of 'phenomenon' as a trouble testifies to the concretisation of the object of analysis.

We have already suggested that bias is a concrete trouble which the social sciences treat as a practical matter. Because 'bias results from the collection of evidence in such a way that an alternative answer to a research question is favoured,[2] it is a threat to objectification, and thus is taken into account in programmes of objectification. Commitment becomes reformulated as favouritism in the positive project. Given the notion that inquestive commitment is an underlying and

[2] C. Sellitz, *et al.*, *Research Methods in the Social Sciences*, rev. ed., New York: Holt, Rinehart and Winston, 1962, p. 50.

constant feature of speech, the positive programme transforms the re-cognition of commitment into the idea of favouritism and therefore poses the problem of eliminating favouritism as the problem of eliminating bias. What we have to grasp is the degeneracy of the move involved in reformulating commitment as favouritism, and the grounds for the notion of favouritism as a trouble. In overt participation observation, for example, the researcher may selectively expose himself to data to the point where he can 'find complete immersion in the system, and subsequent likelihood of biased viewpoint, more difficult to avoid. Limited to his specified role, he may be cut off from valuable channels of information, unable to solicit information not normally accessible to his role without arousing suspicion.'[3] The preferred technique for overcoming selective exposure is the one we should expect: sampling in more than one location and at more than one time. In this way the programme designs itself as a concerted and rigorous method for controlling the influence of favouritism in speech.

Because bias appears as a property of a thing it is also something that can be counted—its thingness means it is capable of showing itself as a unit. Bias can be discriminated and distinguished; its boundaries can be seen. And just as bias can be unitised, so may the ways of control, in that they mechanically and self-sufficiently stand off by themselves. We do not much attend to *how* they could work, to the grounds from which we can suppose that they would work. Even theory has this practical side:[4]

'General theory as a point of departure for specialized work in the social sciences will facilitate the control of the biases of observation and interpretation which are at present fostered by departmentalization of education and research in the social sciences.'

This can only be said because favouritism is seen as leading to the folly of taking what is apparent (to a body, time, place) as what is Real. Here general theory, because it is general and not necessarily linked to anything in particular, will by its very

[3] M. W. Riley, *Sociological Research: I. A Case Approach*, New York: Harcourt, Brace and World, 1963, p. 72.

[4] Talcott Parsons, and Edward Shils, eds, *Toward a General Theory of Action*, New York: Harper and Row, 1962, p. 3.

existence overcome the bias that results from the specialisation of selective approaches to subject matter. Once joined to guides for technique ('is the question content loaded or biased in one direction, without accompanying questions to balance the emphasis? is the wording biased? is it emotionally loaded or slanted toward a particular kind of answer?'[5] etc.) one has, in effect, done all he can to control bias.

Of course one can never claim that bias has been eliminated: 'To be sure, there is no guarantee that any given research undertaking actually will produce relevant, reliable, and unbiased information';[6] or, again, 'We cannot eliminate the effect of the observer in science; we can however, limit and measure this effect and thus gain some control over the variables in the research.'[7] In our terms, bias points to the problem of how to limit and measure the effect of the speaker upon his speech, assuming not only some unexplored limit as ideal, but simultaneously forgetting that any such assessment participates in the very problem it seeks to control by affirming the assessor's effect upon his assessment.

Taking seriously the statements that no guarantees are available and that observer effects cannot be eliminated, we can begin to see the auspices we set out to depict: bias exists in every study, but do not act as if it does. This is necessary because if bias exists in any study, it also exists in any 'solution', thus converting any solution into an icon of its insolubility. We must then forget that the very activity of re-cognising and addressing bias only re-affirms the impossibility of the task. To say 'do not act as if bias exists in every study even though it does' is to intend: exempt this re-cognition from the status of a 'study' (i.e., treat it as a resource). When it is said that bias is a possibility in every study, and that observer effects cannot be eliminated, we should more faithfully say that bias exists in every study—at least, that is what people who specialise in research methods tell us. Our way of saying this is that the positive researcher recognises the omnipresence of commitment in any intelligible speech and poses this as a trouble; he reformulates commitment as the ground of speaking into a notion of the

---

[5] Sellitz, op. cit., pp. 558, 564.

[6] Ibid., p. 2.

[7] W. J. Goode, and Paul Hatt, *Methods of Social Research*, New York: McGraw-Hill, 1952, p. 130.

favouritism of self-interested speaking. Given this reformulation he then sees the imperativeness of a programme for eliminating favouritism. Our question thus, is not whether bias exists but rather how bias exists, how it is ignored in some places, and how it is not ignored in others. What is there about the idea of bias such that it can exist and yet we can act as though it does not? By what *rule* do we accomplish this, in the sense that we are not seeking to depict deviant social scientists, but rather the conventional social scientist—the one who allows always for the possibility of bias, who accepts the fiat that it can be controlled but not eliminated, and who yet selectively notices the existence of bias in some cases but not in others. Seeing bias is a rule-guided procedure, not a random one. But it should be clear now that seeing bias is not simply a matter of calling attention to an intrinsic property of some research report, since it is said to exist in every research report for one thing, and because it must be warranted in some way, for another. So what *is* taken into account such that it can generate the charge of bias in some cases, and inhibit the charge in others? How in other words, does the behaviour of social scientists on this question display for us the concerted ways in which their fundamental principles organise their evaluations? Though favouritism is an omnipresent feature of speech it can be ignored in some cases and the problem becomes one of orienting to favouritism and operating upon it in such a way as to make its irrelevancy credible to a collective. The positive solution: since the idea that commitment grounds every speech cannot be reconciled with the intention to 'reduce it' (since the intention denies the re-cognition by treating a parameter as if it could be otherwise), differentiate the commitment underlying the re-cognition (by not bringing it into question) from the commitment that *is* re-cognised (the commitment discernible in the study that *is* re-cognised) by calling the latter self-interest.

If bias exists in every study it cannot be apparent because to recognise it in *this* case, and to tolerate it in *that*, is to have a special sense of 'tolerable limit' which permits (or sanctions the permitting of) some committed talk to go unnoticed (i.e., to be treated as not displaying favouritism and self-interest). Such decisions confirm the fact that bias is not an 'apparent' predicate of things. The possibility of bias talk presupposes a very sophisticated conception of trouble (in this sense, a conception which itself invites attention to itself as a trouble). Yet, while the concern of social scientists with bias indicates that it is anything but apparent, their speeches about it all presuppose its determinate status as an appearance.

III. BIAS AS A NORMAL TROUBLE

Because bias is a parameter of evaluation if not of studies, our problem is to understand bias as that sort of normal trouble in the regular activities of social science. In order to accomplish this we shall have to construct a form of life which guides sociologists in their organisation of intelligible speech about bias. Bias in this sense is a move in some game, and in order to understand that move we must first know the rules by which it can come to life, sensibly and within the terms of the game.

The practical conception of bias which is employed in the social sciences is not then to be proven incorrect or wrong by our analysis. An analytic conception of bias should make reference to the socially organised understandings which provide for any intelligible use of the concept. It will not demonstrate when it is appropriate to invoke bias anew. It will not serve as a decision procedure for helping us to estimate bias in practical situations. In this sense our analytic conception will take as its problem the act of evaluation itself and the assumption brought to bear on the situation by the ideal evaluator.

We have begun with the ordinary surface practices of members in producing the idea of bias as a troublesome thing. In this respect, bias is not the deep grounds of the decision, bias *is* the decision. We address this usage in order to locate the deep set of understandings and conventions which provide for the intelligibility of usage. An analytic treatment of bias should seek to delineate the corpus of knowledge employed by a typical member to accomplish his recognition of a report as biased. It is our task to organise what is commonly described as bias according to the grounds which make these descriptions intelligible. That is to say, bias has already been described as a troublesome thing in that it is conceived to manifest itself at the point where questions are constructed, behaviours are sampled, observations are recorded. It is in this regard a constraint or order to which the investigator must be oriented in his inquiry.

Its elimination or control is not only a normatively desirable element of inquiry, but a precondition of any claim to knowledge itself, and so is deeply grounded in the most fundamental rules in social science. It is these grounds that make our conventional speech about bias intelligible and which we shall attempt to depict.

The question is: what kind of trouble appears omnipresent? Since that which is omnipresent can only be a trouble if it is concretised, the very notion of trouble makes reference to a concrete understanding of speech. Where speech is a thing (where it copies nature) there should be no favouritism because it is assumed to be oriented to in the same way by all; it is shared, not idiosyncratic. Such speech is expected to demonstrate that the time-space locality of the speaker is irrelevant to what he speaks about. Nature is assumed as an object present to all if they abandon constraints of locality. Description of nature is undertaken in order to create speech under the auspices of the image of relevance (not vice versa); all can be in the same position to hear. To charge bias is to accuse one of not attending to this requisite. He must then orient to the standard of concretising speech so as to produce equality (and he must think of speech in the most concrete terms). To say bias is omnipresent is then to say that commitment is omnipresent, and to say bias is a trouble is to say that commitment is a 'trouble', a conception which is only intelligible through a positive project of speaking which sees commitment as caprice, self-interest and idiosyncratic rather than as grounds. Further, to see commitment as trouble is to exempt the recognition of 'seeing commitment as a trouble' as a display of the selfsame trouble. Commitment is then seen as a trouble because it is reinterpreted as favouritism and consequently as that which prevents community and equality. The equality of speech is treated as the only authentic disclosure of what is. Yet, the act of re-cognising the trouble is not itself seen as a trouble—as the same trouble—because *this* re-cognition expresses the undifferentiated unity of the one who sees with his community via their unexplored togetherness. The unproblematic nature of the re-cognition of the trouble denies the thesis of the omnipresence of the trouble. This is necessary for two reasons: (1) an omnipresent trouble is a parameter—not a trouble—and cannot be 'acted upon' and (2) if the act of recognition is not discriminated from that which it re-cognises its claim would lose its force as grounds for the identification and reduction of bias because the act would be a further affirmation of bias itself. The act would become a programmatic demonstration of the impossibility of the programme.

The re-cognition of bias absolutely requires as its ground the observer's differentiation of self from that about which he speaks (the old subject–object split) because *his* re-cognition must be exempted from scrutiny. Bias talk presupposes a descriptivist form of life which in turn requires this differentiation. Otherwise description would lose its force and the 'object' would only reappear as an extension of the 'subject's' authority, as an icon of his commitment.

IV. DEEP STRUCTURE OF BIAS

The very existence of the surface behaviour of bias and of bias-discredited work is made possible by positivism, without which no such thing as bias could exist as we know it. This is not to say that commitment would not be recognised or that the trouble of commitment would not be recognised. But without positivism we would be without positivism's method of speaking about commitment as the troubles of favouritism. As a rule-violation, bias is itself in accord with a deeper rule, the rule of positivism which is organised around particular notions of speech, nature, community, and in this case, commitment. The troublesomeness of bias is not something that just happens to be the case (say because there are many dishonest or poorly trained researchers around) but rather bias is a necessary product of a positive conception of science. The concretisation of commitment as the trouble that is favouritism is a product of a way of thinking about speech that we have come to call science. This sense of favouritism is only possible where self is concretised as self-centredness and where being committed is seen as 'private' or 'capricious', and this only follows from a notion that speech ought to be impersonal (de-authored) in order to show the anonymity of its source. The act of re-cognising the trouble must, then, show the ideal of anonymity which the 'object' of such a re-cognition is seen to offend.

In so far as bias offends the notion of objectivity, whatever presupposes the possibility of objectivity (like the positive project) also presupposes the possibility of bias. This is to say that the intelligibility of bias as a charge or accusation makes necessary reference to the rule which the charge violates, and the rule in this case is a notion of objectivity which is itself grounded in an ideal of communality and of impersonal speech. The ideal is displayed in the very act of re-cognising bias. Although it might be said that positivism is meant to reduce the existence of concretely biased reports, so does positivism generate the possibility of such reports precisely by setting out to eliminate them. In this sense bias shows not just violation, but rule. In this sense bias is not only a problem which positivism sets out to resolve but is created and produced as a problem by the very project which sets out to solve it. This is why Nietzsche could say of science, as he said of Christianity that it is the priests who invent illness, that it is the rule which invents the exception.

The deep structures which generate the possibility of bias are (1) rules for charging bias, (2) the theoretic community of members in which bias may occur, and (3) a grammar by which members of the community recognise bias and the particular instances of its appearance. It remains for us to describe these structures for two reasons. First, they serve as special moves or displays in the language game of positivism. Second, they reveal our method of analysis, namely that any behaviour of sociological interest can be conceived to have its analysable source in some community of members' identification and use of rules. With regard to the latter point, we are suggesting that our analysis of bias can reveal (1) the language game in which bias is an intelligible act, i.e., that which makes favouritism an intelligible charge; (2) our own language game by which the intelligibility of any set of concrete activities can be transformed into its own language game, i.e., our commitment which enables us to *hear* bias as a confirmation of favouritism, and favouritism itself as a corruption of the idea of commitment. We analyse bias as one move in a positivist game, and in so doing we aim to provide a display of our own game.

Bias is a counterclaim, i.e., it cannot be understood solely by making reference to the claim of the charger. To understand bias requires seeing it originally as not merely dependent upon, but as necessitating the form of the first claim which itself offers the possibility of its own bias or counterclaim. This is to say that it is not just in the concrete observer's or charger's formulation that one can understand the idea of bias, even though this is where such a possibility surfaces.

Any claim at all then, including the original materials to which bias is charged, contains the very possibility of the charge, a possibility which may or may not work out to be followed by some concrete accusation. This is to say that the possibility of bias necessarily requires that it be charged to something, which in turn makes that something itself vulnerable to the charge.

Another way of saying this: the standards to which the charger of bias makes reference in the course of his charge themselves involve the kind and form of materials to which the charge might be applied. The first question thus becomes not what is a charge of bias, but rather to what sorts of materials can the charge be levelled? Or, again, to what sorts of materials are observers oriented as displays of their notions of claims to adequacy? This generates a universe of things which contain the possibility that they could be attacked for bias. This generates a universe of speeches as things of which bias could be predicated.

The first 'obvious' aspect of biased materials is their inadequacy, of course. We must begin with the rules and method for conceiving of this inadequacy, and in order to understand this we must first understand what an adequate inquiry, or knowing is:[8]

> If someone says he *knows* something, it must be something that, by general consent, he is in a position to know.

Knowing thus becomes a treatment of an individual which invests him with knowledge 'by general consent'. Agreement must be elicited, for knowing to be seen as an appropriate treatment. This then is a usage notion of knowing, because being in a position to know something means being present to what one speaks about, i.e., it recommends that what one speaks about is present in a particular way to the one who does the speaking. This notion will be seen to generate the idea of favouritism because if one has privileged access to what he speaks about and if the claim to know contains as a parameter

[8] Ludwig Wittgenstein, *On Certainty*, New York: Harper, 1969, p. 73.

the claim of such privileged access, a trouble for research is generated, in the sense that the speech that is made must be segregated from its concrete author and treated as a speech of anyman. Speech must be divested of its privilege, but only under the assumption that privilege makes reference to the special access which the concrete speaker has to what he speaks.

The methods proposed by social scientists show through their procedures the belief in the necessity of agreement for the proper doing of science. As men in the game of science, they must decide when to evoke the rule of bias. It can be stated that natural science seeks to locate within nature properties that warrant the accreditation of the description as invariant; indeed the thrust of Wittgenstein's point is that one should *read* invariance as equivalent to agreement or 'general consent'. Regarding this necessity of science Harré notes that:[9]

> Invariances are not all obvious in nature, and cannot be demonstrated in any obvious way by experiment. It is not clear how one would demonstrate experimentally that momentum is conserved in a certain sort of interaction. This cannot be done by separating off the momentum and measuring it independently of the bodies which 'possess' it; for momentum is the product of mass and velocity and these are quite different sorts of bodily property. Clearly the origin of the invariances is not to be found in the experimental side of science. It is to be found in the general conceptual system.

Even if this is the undergirding of science, what light is then shed on the nature of bias as one rule of science? In the scientific community bias is a way of seeing the intrusion of irrelevant interest into an inquiry where the notion of irrelevance is defined, ironically enough, as that which is most relevant to the speaker, i.e., as that which he has an interest in preserving and aggrandising. What he has an interest in preserving is the illusion that his privileged access to his speech is irrelevant. Bias points to the scientist's version of the problem of suspicion, because to charge bias is to indicate that one is suspicious of the speaker's claim that his authorship (authority) is irrelevant.

But there are many interests which science deems irrelevant,

[9] R. Harré, *Matter and Method*, London: Macmillan & Co., 1964, p. 32.

so our next question concerns which sorts of interest are those which represent bias? We shall propose that bias is the intrusion of unnecessary personal interests which fall outside of what are conceived to be the inevitable consequences of history and character. To see bias is to see the purported inquiry as more intelligible by making reference to the contingent personal position of the inquirer than to the nature of the objects he claims to describe. Bias rests on the notion that these personal auspices of the inquirer make it impossible for him to locate invariances and thus no comparison of 'findings' is possible. 'Comparison of findings' is of course, a positivist metaphor for fellowship and for the social relationship, and in this sense the charge of bias is grounded in a conception of adequate speech which stipulates rational speech to be the speech which demonstrates its interchangeability for anyman. Consequently, the idea of favouritism affirms the re-cognition that the speech demonstrates not fellowship but self-interest. To recognise that the speech demonstrates self-interest rather than the ideal of fellowship is itself a display of fellowship.

Simply to assert that personal character enters a description is not enough, however. Not everything that displays character is of itself vulnerable to the charge of bias. Think of art, dreams, aptitudes, attitudes, preferences, food, as displays of character. It is thus probably not just showing character, or the accusation that one has shown his, which displays bias, since it is not applied to these forms of character display. Notice that we typically conceive these things to be possibilities in a different way than bias. Bias is *only* a possibility, established by making a certain kind of claim. Bias is a contingency. It is not necessary, not inevitable, the way having dreams or preferences is inevitable. Bias is conventional in the technical sense of the term, i.e., we think it need not occur. This means it cannot be applied to (distortions caused by) basic character or history. When by perspective we mean historical perspective, we do not charge bias. We talk instead about controlling bias, since it cannot be eliminated. One confusion of the literature is thus clarified by distinguishing between 'unnecessary' and 'necessary' observer effects (effects that are treated as being one or the other).

Living in history, as opposed to living in bias, has got to be an inevitable feature of any enquiry; Mannheim not to the

E

contrary, history and its effects are thought to be beyond the resources of the individual inquirer. To fail in historical terms is to be wrong, and not biased. So there is still something elusive about bias, in that while it is contingent it is not the kind of contingent we would call wrong. It is not to be mistaken. To be mistaken means to be able to be forgiven. Yet bias is a charge that brooks no forgiveness, it is not that kind of mistake. Bias is unavoidable in some way that does not permit us to forgive it. Perhaps it has something to do with intent (which is absent in mistakes). Perhaps it shows self-aggrandisement and the repudiation of the standard of equality, in the sense that man puts himself above nature and hence above community (see below, 'will').

The material to which bias can be applied, and also wrongness or mistakenness, make a claim to have seen something or to propose something constative, in that something must be acceded: the claim must be granted before it is 'complete'. That is, as with bias, the original must be understood to incorporate that it needs agreement or rejection. This is a necessary feature of a constative claim. Corny statements like 'if I have seen further. . . .' are not entirely undescriptive. One element of these materials is that as one claims to have seen something, someone else may claim to have seen further—not just differently—as in historical epochs or through preferences and attitudes, but further. This is interesting because it indicates that positivism as the source of the possibility of bias is not just summarised by the old idea of the constative, but also by the segregation of it from other forms of life and by conceiving it as having its own stretching and narrowing, its own regular and orderly elasticity. One can, within the constative be short- or far-sighted. The charger is claiming to see further. He is claiming to see something that the author (agent) did not. But it is not just to see more, like distinguishing major and minor figures in a discipline or some such thing. It is not to see more facts or more truths or more constatives. Nor is it to see truths more deeply. What is not seen is this: that the unity of man and nature is disclosed as a difference between speech and its grounds, where these grounds are the things which speech speaks about.

Here, finally, we come upon the difference between mistakes and biases. The former concern more and/or deeper constatives or different ones. Bias is something else. Bias concerns ignorance of one's private or personal auspices, and the failure to make those auspices publicly methodic. In positivism one's auspices must be demonstrated as the 'things' external to speech. That is, the only legitimate commitment permissible in the positive project is to things external to speech rather than to the grounds of speech. Since it is impossible for speech to be grounded in speeches (intelligible objects) external to speech, the project transforms grounds as commitment into the evil of self-interest.

Think for a moment of the presumably public feature of science in its connection to bias. Harré notes on this point that science demands qualities:[10]

> which persist through each process separately, and there must be those which persist in repetition so that rules can be applied. We say 'must' here, not because there is some universal necessity which forces these invariances upon us, but because the nature of our science is determined by our choice of invariants. [He also asserts that] prediction depends upon having a rule which usually works; to have a rule it is necessary that it be applied successfully more than once. But for there to be a second application of a rule there must be some invariance either in process, substance, or property which persists from the first application of a rule to the second and the subsequent applications, as the invariance of momentum is a characteristic of mechanical changes.

Prediction demands public consent in the recognition of a common factor which could be located in a succession of cases. Bias fouls prediction, theoretically, because it designates a researcher and a set of findings which can be seen in successive cases only if the theories of the particular researcher are respected. Thus the public, consensual character of the inquiry is violated; it is personalised. To see bias is to see the inquirer using the work as a method of making reference to *his* 'irrelevant interest', which is very different from saying that he made a mistake. The point to be stressed here is that of the intentionality assumed by the evaluator, who must see the evaluated member as oriented to self and to standards which are regarded

10 Harré, ibid., p. 33.

as unnecessarily personal for the investigative purposes at hand. In orienting to one's own interest as a resource for study one is failing to respond to the necessity of promoting some authoritative version of the world which is intelligible to a community; a biased researcher is assumed to be showing an inability to control his interests where the object(s) of such interests are matters external to the objects about which he claims to speak.

Thus within the positive project the charge of bias is really a charge that the inquirer is showing lack of reflexivity because he is deflected from respecting community and this deflection is created by forces over which he has no intellectual control, i.e., by will. Bias is then inadequate inquiry in the following sense: it is to fail out of ignorance (of one's unnecessarily private auspices), to be a theoretic member of the scientific community of agreement. It is to base a public claim upon the private. It is not to possess the private (attitudes, biography), but to transliterate the private into the public without knowing it.

The charger thus claims to have seen further, because the original claim to see is only private and not publicly available (not capable of being seen). Whatever the original claim contains can in this view never be more than ostensibly the case. This does sound like character, attitude, etc., but it is not. While bias is private, it is not private in the way that character is private (as a result of what one person possesses) so much as what one *failed to wish*. Up to this point we have bias as a claim to be able to see further because the original claim devolves from the private, and whatever is seen this way is irrelevant because it is unshareable. Now it is being suggested that bias is a particular kind of privacy, namely the kind of privacy that could be shaken off or suspended. To be biased is not to suffer the inevitable such as character or history. It is rather to 'choose'. Perhaps this accounts for the inspection of the motives of the agent of biased products, i.e., of seeing the claim as faulty-with-a-reason. The charge that something is biased, then, is to charge that the inquirer *could have seen further if he wanted to*. It is a display of the various positivist auspices such as the non-personal, the natural, self-control of will, the distinction between mind (will and the private) and body (observation and the public) etc. Bias also displays the notion that while social structure (character, history) can erect barriers to objectification, it also permits the exercise of choice in accomplishing objectification. The problem of bias then, poses the question of the role of self in inquiry and the very intelligibility of the charge rests upon a version of language and self that is quite decisive and particular.

To be biased is to accept too many limits, assuming the private is a limit. Needless to say, anything unformulable is made impossible here, in the sense that the unformulable would be private and 'unimportant'—irrelevant to understanding. More, the unformulable is thought to get in the way of understanding and this reflects the positivist theory of observer as automaton democrat: if you ignore character and exercise the typical will, you will accomplish a description. Auspices are seen as democratic in the sense that disinterested theory is conducted through typically wilful disembodiments.

The public character of science is the equivalent of a community of theoretic members capable of agreement. When we fail to see community in an inquiry we are expected, according to the rules of the scientific language game, to look for his private interests as the means for understanding his inquiry. When we find such interests, we are charging bias. The grammar of bias is thus to see the researcher reporting to *us* rather than to any member of the community.

This brings us around to the essential feature of science as 'what anyone could know'. Any scientific claim can now be seen as a procedure for generating that. 'What anyone could know' refers not to whether anyone *does* know, but that they could know. That is, if only they ignore the influence of character on history, and have the will to see beyond their own interest, they could know. This is what is meant by training in method and so forth, which is training to ignore certain aspects of self and time and to suspend other interests. Naturalism makes knowledge there for the public asking. Biased researchers are thus the ones who do not know and who fail to inform us of what they and we could know, because they wilfully reject the public auspices of community by wilfully invoking unnecessarily private auspices. These grounds for charging bias are themselves dependent upon the democratic individualism which is typical of positivistic versions of inquiry.

In summary, our method has been to depict bias as a rule in the scientific language game which has its own grammar. Our method leads us to see that it is grounded in the community of science in so far as scientists can be seen concertedly to apply the idea. According to its rule, bias is first of all *noticeable*, in the sense that it is a thing which can appear to the audience, even though it does not appear in the way history does. Furthermore, since it need not appear, we assume that the one so charged would have to be doing it wilfully in the sense that he is rejecting the theoretic standard which any member of the scientific community can apply. And what appears to us as the grammar of bias is the private, as the only way to understand the report. Bias is thus (1) a rule-guided charge in the (2) theoretic community of science with a (3) grammar of the unnecessarily private, i.e., of the extraneous and irrelevant.

V. THE POSITIVIST RATIONALE FOR BIAS

Having provided our conception of the deep rules for positivist conceptions of bias according to their rule, theoretic community and grammar, we could have considered our task to be complete. But we would then fail to depict our own grounds for so characterising positivist conceptions, grounds which we conceive to be very different than positivist ones. That is, we would claim that a positivist could not have produced the description we have just offered because that description was generated by a different method of analysis. While we have shown this idea throughout the previous sections we will now proceed to concretise what we have shown through a more particular characterisation.

For clarity's sake, let us briefly explicate at least three levels of meaning for 'bias':

1. The possibilities available to anyone at any time as the activity 'bias'.
2. Positivists' use of 'bias'.
3. Our idea of 'bias'.

The positivists take one line, or kind of possibility, in (1) and formulate (2). (3) is a limiting case of both (1) and (2). (3) formulates (2) in the sense that it depicts those uses for which positivists can be held responsible in that we claim an observer could (we have) intelligibly impute it to them. We can hold the positivists responsible in so far as there is an under-lying intelligibility to our imputation.

When we say we are treating bias as a positivist's method for displaying his conception of adequate inquiry, we are really also saying that we are using our conception of bias (3) to refer to our idea of the positivist conception of bias (2). Examine the difference between

(a) I shall treat bias as a positivist's method for displaying his conception of knowledge and,

(b) I shall treat bias as my idea of bias. My idea of bias refers to my idea of the positivist's conception of bias.

Is the object of (a) different from the object of (b)? If we began the investigation under the auspices of (a) would we be looking at different things than if we conduct it under (b)?

Assuming that the difference between (a) and (b) is grammatical, and represents a different analytic authority, we can say that whatever the similarity or dissimilarity of the object between (a) and (b), what we are looking at becomes intelligible only by making reference to the auspices of the (b) kind of analysis we invoke. We can, in other words, make reference to our own version of an authoritative analysis while constructing the authority for a positivist's use of bias. Without an explication of our own version of positivism, the content of our description of bias is only one alternative among several, in the sense that no authority for seeing it our way is provided. Bias has a place in our analysis as a method of making reference to our auspices, and has a place in the positivist's activity as a method of making reference to his auspices. The difference is that for the positivist user bias is a resource, where for us it is a topic. His is meant to describe something, where for us bias serves only as an example of a certain kind of analysis (our kind). We can probably succeed in displaying our authority if we can produce an understanding of how bias (or any other activity) is an example rather than a description. And we have already done that to a degree, in so far as we have generated an idea of bias that in no way includes the 'accuracy' of the charge in particular cases. Bias as we see it can never be linked to the 'truth' if by that is meant that either the essential feature or any other feature of bias is whether the materials to which it is charged are in fact biased. This would be description, a determining interest in the empirical validity of the label. We, on the other hand, have tried to show the auspices of bias in so far as those auspices generate the eventual concrete activities of bias charging and biased reports. In our formulation the charges in the report are only examples of the auspices. (Positivist rules, the positivist theoretic community, the positivist grammar of bias.) Our kind of analysis, then requires an explication of the grounds of some activity, not a concrete description of it. We do not reject bias, but we make its claim transparent by showing how it rests upon a particular version of knowledge and how this version of knowledge formulates adequate speech as speech which accurately describes things.

Given that we have so far only provided a picture of the auspices of bias *through* our auspices—the analysis up to now is a display of our authority, to be sure, but it is not a delineation of the authority itself—what else is to be done? We can begin more certainly to provide that authority (it is probably impossible ever to fully characterise) by more carefully making reference to our auspices on the same topic. We have drawn a picture of bias. Bias has been portrayed as an example of positivism. The question now becomes, how do we provide for such a user? How does this rational inquirer we have just invented use bias as an icon of some authority?

The first point to grasp is that the need for a conception of bias is only intelligible within a particular tradition. Speech in this tradition acquired its intelligibility within an intellectual context in which opinion was taken for knowledge, and where, consequently, differences in opinion, appearances, impressions, and so forth, were identical with differences in knowledge. In other words, this is a tradition that identified opinion with knowledge. The use of bias makes reference to the essential variability of opinion and thus to the problem of what can be taken for knowledge. As an attempt to solve the problem of indexicality and variability, it requires concretising the idea of knowledge. If knowledge is opinion (essentially), and if opinions are indexically tied for their sense and use to the occasions of their accomplishment, then knowledge is in this tradition going to be a *political* question, in that it will have to be negotiated through persuasion and agreement. The use of bias is a method for making reference to this kind of context.

What precisely is the problem within the kind of context just described? That the indexicality of speech—its situated character—makes perfect speech impossible, when the image of perfect speech is perfectly concrete speech, speech which fulfils concrete notions of perfectibility such as total finite characterisation. Yet according to positivism perfect concrete speech is still a possible achievement and one that can be accomplished with some method. Positivism's perfect speech would be speech that normalises its essential indexicality, which makes this essential indexicality a *trouble* for members. Bias becomes in this context a way of anticipating and detecting that trouble.

Note for example, that when Socrates faced an interlocutor who was incompetent, for example a Meno or Polus, he did not make the charge of bias, but they did. They said that no one would agree with him, that his speech was his own and not that of any man, and so on. Now, if his speech was 'his own'—if as Protagoras says, 'man is the measure'—Socrates' speech should have been allowed to stand merely through its accomplishment. Plato identified the problem here by pointing out that if 'every man is the measure', how can any man's speech be discredited? To put it another way: how can any man induce the other to accept his speech, since it would be wrong for other compared to other's own speech, which would be right for him? If knowledge is the equivalent of opinion, and if opinion is essentially indexical, then truth is indexically connected to the speechmaker. One might say Socrates is correct (for him), and the other is correct (for him), but Plato pointed out that if it were consistently followed this conclusion (anarchy) would not provide any speaker with grounds for speaking. Another way of saying this is if knowledge and appearance are identified and if appearance is essentially connected to becoming and perspectiviality, then truth is equivalent to what appears, and what appears only appears to a particular perspective: therefore perspectives cannot be surpassed. In other words, there would be no rule of adequacy. Consequently, in this Protagorean *cum* positivist culture, adequacy comes to inducing the other to agree through persuasion (read: scientific method). Given the problem which the conception of knowledge as opinion generates for itself, adequacy comes to be a kind of forceful bringing-into-line. In this regard bias is one of the worst things one could say about a speech (about an opinion) because it is to assert the anarchic forcelessness of that speech.

To say 'every man is the measure' is therefore to open yourself to the question of what kind of measure a man is: if every man is the measure, this means that any single, particular man, in order to be seen as an adequate measure, has to be the measure of all men or of any man. Any single man has to typify the hypothetical concrete community of men. So, the anarchy of Protagorean positivism—every man the measure—eventually has to be resolved through a collective solution: that the best man (measure) is the man who is the measure of any man. This is nice, because the best man is the man who typifies the community: the collective. The best man is the *one* who shows the many (public) in himself: the best man (measure) is the man who shows community (the public).

Take all of this so far as a kind of elliptical sketch of a context for bias talk. It is a context in which the speech of one is to be the speech of any man. So the one who charges bias is saying in effect, 'I cannot participate in your speech and I should be able to.' That is, your speech is supposed to be my speech (any man's speech), so what I charge you with is that it is only *your* speech. To say bias is to say that your speech is not the speech of any man; it is distinctively your speech; speech which is (analytically) owned by the public is here no more than your private possession, i.e., it is owned by you. Thus, the charge is that your speech, which is communal property despite the fact of your particular authorship, appears in its accomplishment as if it is private property.

This is a form of life where the speech which you concretely perform is analytically a speech of any man, so when bias is charged, you are being accused of identifying the concrete (your own speech) with the analytic (any man's public speech). It is an assertion that the speaker treats the concrete fact that he *happens* to be the speaker as an analytic formulation. This is the positivist way of calling someone concrete and it displays the positivist analytic of grounded speech.

To charge bias is then a positivistic way of saying that the speech is not analytic, because for the positivist, the analytic character of the speech consists in its status as speech authored by nature. In positivism nature is the speaker, nature makes the speech. In this sense nature is the real author although the inquirer is concretely the one who puts the words together. To see bias is to say that the speech is not analytic because it is not authored by nature (by what ought be its real author), but by the concrete speaker. It is almost as if the concrete speaker has tampered with the speech, which is an offence against the laws of community since he is only supposed to imitate and copy and not to innovate. Analytic speech is speech which is seen as authored by nature; concrete speech is speech which is seen as authored by the concrete speaker, or as speech which is seen as interfered with by the concrete speaker in such a way as to conceal its real authorship.

To say that the concrete speaker is the author is a way of saying that the speaker is concrete, so when a positivist says that the speech he hears is not analytic, he is saying he has grounds for deciding that it is not authored by nature. Analytic speech is speech that makes reference to its authorial auspices in nature. The notion of author here formulates the way in which the source of speech is located and responsibility for speech is assigned. The author is something like the fundamental cause, and so, deciding authorship is deciding authority for the speech. It is a way of making some (one) thing responsible for the speech, which is nature in positivism. Furthermore it shows the kind of author that nature is: nature is a thing, an external, discrete thing which is to be imitated. The thingness of nature resides in its externality and in its coerciveness (in Durkheim's sense it coerces because the inquirer is compelled to imitate it in speeches). The thingness of nature also makes reference to its undifferentiated character in the sense that as a thing it is a thing to be recorded as a one. Accurate speech must then record and preserve the oneness and thingness of this undifferentiated external nature, and in so far as speeches vary and differ among themselves we have a hint that the oneness has not been observed (preserved).

If man is the measure, then there is no way of allocating authority differentially to speeches (to men) because all are equally authoritative. Authority then has to be conceived as that which is responsible for making something out of nothing, for making speech. Authority is assigned to the author of the speech, and this author cannot be the man but must be nature. If nature is responsible (is the author) then differences between concrete speakers should cancel out and speakers *should* agree. When speakers fail to agree, it can be decided (1) that nature is not the author, and (2) that the speech is not authoritative, because (3) the author is the concrete speaker, i.e., is speaking under the auspices of private self-centred interest. Thus, to say that the speaker rather than nature is responsible (the author) is to say that speech is not authoritative—it is only concrete.

Therefore, within the context of positivist auspices, the concrete speaker is not an author; he is a one through whom the analytic author—nature—speaks. Nature speaks through the speaker.

In positivism, the speaker is a vehicle of nature, his analytic status is that of a messenger. The inquirer is not an author; he passes the word but he does not author it. This is to say that the inquirer does not create the word, because he merely passes it on from its creator. He is not responsible for originating the word, he is responsible only for transmitting it.

An inadequate inquirer, now a poor messenger, is one who gets it wrong, distorts it and so on. But how can we tell, since we never have a direct confrontation with the author in positivism? We can only hear through nature's messengers and yet it is only through those messengers that one can decide the adequacy of the message. The way to decide if we have a straight message is by a conception of the messenger as an adequate messenger: an adequate messenger is one who is an instrument or a tool, in the sense that to be a messenger is to be nature's mouthpiece. An instrument is a kind of near-at-hand piece of unproblematic recording equipment. If the most serious charge is that the author's (nature's) speech has been tampered with and responsibility for the speech has been arrogated by the speaker, then the adequate speaker is a facsimile of nature's record. The adequate speaker must personify nature itself by speaking in a natural way, by making his speech into a thing (into another item of nature).

The inadequate speaker comes to be a problem in positivism because he undermines the possibility of the community, of the public. The community hangs together because nature reveals itself honestly; nature is no deceiver. The problem, then, is not the problem of nature but of man: will man follow the proper steps as the canons of adequate messengership? These methods—of man—are technical operations which he shares with all men. What separates men is how they use such instruments. Do they use the instrument as an instrument, do they use the instrument analytically? Or do they subjugate it to the self, do they use it concretely? Do they use the instrument in the service of something higher—nature—or do they use the instrument in the service of their pleasure—their concrete self-interest? To use an instrument as an instrument is to pass on nature's speech without altering it. To subjugate it to the self is to misuse the instrument or technique by assimilating it to one's own interests and purposes, letting it become too important in life, assigning 'meaning' to it which is not publicly required, thinking about it too much, and so forth. To be adequate the instrument must be used solely in terms of rational efficiency: getting the speech straight and across, as clocks tell the time of day. To say bias is thus to say that the speech shows aggrandisement on the part of the speaker, that he is not a reliable messenger. It is to require that the hearer make reference to the speaker as well as to the speech. The speaker is seen as having no control or discipline. It is the trust-worthy and reliable character of the messenger that mediates the link between nature and the community. A good messenger knows his place as one who does not intervene and knows that the speech he delivers should not make reference to the concrete self who does the delivering.

In positivism, to say that the speaker is biased is to say that the speech is not authoritative (not analytic) because it does not issue from nature. We cannot trust the speech; while it is intelligible, it is of no help in providing an understanding of nature. The positivist accepts as a given that we desire to control nature because we distinguish ourselves from nature by surpassing it through thinking. The only way to control nature is through understanding. Since nature authors the speeches of men, we want to use the speeches as a way of describing nature. Biased speeches prevent such understanding because they speak to us falsely about nature. Because we want to know truly about nature, our first job is to discriminate good speeches from bad, adequate messengers from inadequate ones, and one way to do so is to generate the possibility of bias.

Bias is produced—it is recognised, charged, attributed, identified in this case but not in that. On every occasion of its production, the achievement of bias talk points beyond the talk itself to the idea from which it devolved. But it is not a determinant essence—some idea-of-bias-as bias—which grounds the talk because any idea of bias is implicated so essentially into an image of perfectibility which bias is seen to offend; bias talk points to an organised cluster of auspices that articulate around some further image of adequate speech.

The grounds of speech—whether bias speech or any other—are not a thing (are no-thing) because grounds are not things. Commitment to grounds is an attachment to no-thing (but not to nothing). It is a commitment to something that is no-thing, something not a thing, to the foundation or Reason which is not itself another thing.

When we make transparent the commitment which underlies bias talk we see it as an attachment to some image of the grounds of speech that identify grounds as some thing (and not no-thing). Underlying this speech is an image of adequate speech as that speaking which ought produce a thing to which speakers could orient in such univocal and standard ways as to guarantee the exclusion of extraneous influences from the speech. This notion of adequate speech requires the control of any influence which could prevent the treatment of speech as a thing. The communal relationship symbolised in the 'ability to compare findings' (and to transform speech into a communal 'topic' of ordinary conversation) is re-presented in the creation of speech that appears as a product, as a concrete and discrete thing which stands to the speaker in a relationship of externality and independence. Since this is the only kind of speech that can be compared and assessed (that can be exchanged), forces which mitigate against its creation will be seen as anti-social.

Given the positive project's concrete conception of sociality as exchange, the anti-social possibility of speech is shown, or appears, through speech which looks expressive rather than descriptive. Yet since all speech can look expressive, because speaking is essentially founded in interest, aspiration, and anticipation, the positive programme discriminates between speech which expresses the unity of speaker and nature (the unity called the description) and speech which announces the difference between speaker and nature.

The charge of bias points to the difference between speaker and nature under the assumption that such differentiation discloses the fragmentation of a unity which ought to underlie the image of adequate speech. Such differentiation then discloses that the standard of adequate speech has been offended. Such differentiation is 'seen' as follows: that the impulses of the speaker overcame him and prevented him from preserving the unity of the relationship between speaker and nature because of his vulnerability to pressures of self-centredness.

The tension in the positive programme is reflected in the discrepancy between the standard of anonymity which underlies the positive image of communal speech and the formulation of the speaker as one who (naturally) desires to maximise his difference. The natural man is then seen as one who finds it impossible to live up to the standard of anonymity. Method is a device for inducing the speaker to accept his communal responsibility and the recognition of bias as a trouble is (deeply) the recognition of the danger of vanity (and of the reformulation of the human as the vain and self-centred organism of seventeenth-century thought). The recognition of the omnipresence of bias is a symptom of the uneasy recognition that the very standard of anonymous speech can be seen to deny itself on any occasion of its accomplishment because of the essential humanity of language. The ideal of eliminating bias suggests the interest in forgetting the human parameter in order to create an approximation in speech to that which the standard recommends as ideal.

Speech which demonstrates its faithfulness to the standard of anonymity is speech which makes reference to its togetherness with nature where nature is itself understood as those *things* which can be produced through speech. Thus, speech is at one with nature when it is at one with it-self, i.e., when it speaks so as to make it-self (itself as speech) an instance of the ideal of speech *as* nature (as a thing). Reliable speech is speech which makes it-self a thing, it is speech that becomes the kind of thing that nature is (a natural thing). Speech shows its faithfulness to its own conception of its unity with the nature it has created for it-self when it constitutes it-self as the kind of thing which (it conceives that) nature is.

Since reliable speech is speech that constitutes itself as a natural thing, this constitution has to be organised as an accomplishment. Therefore in showing its unity with nature, positive speech also shows its superiority, for it (unlike nature) can show its own constitution as the organised becoming that is method. The thing that is positive speaking, unlike the thing it imitates, shows its very activity of imitating as the orderly emergence of a natural thing. If the good speech imitates nature—if it is the natural speech—the very activity of imitating nature is constituted as an other natural thing. The speech becomes an other item in the environment of things called nature, and this is what the notion of a description intends: the reliable description, as the speech to which men can orient as things, guarantees the achievement of the social relationship of science because it is only such speeches that can be compared, assessed, and distributed as products.

Bias talk then presupposes a notion of hoarding which it assumes to be antithetical to an ideal of sharing. It is further assumed that this ideal is exemplified in speech which controls its production by constituting itself under the auspices of an order of exchangeable speech. Such an order affirms the positive ideal of community.

The positive programme formulates this order as the ideal because it identifies the nature of the human with self-centredness, i.e., it commits itself to a view of man as one who essentially hides his interest from others on the grounds of the advantageous consequences of such evasion. Because adequate speech is wrested through the contest between hoarding and sharing, and since man the hoarder will never voluntarily share (in the positive image), a sovereign (method) is required to compel men to make their grounds assessable. To make grounds of speaking assessable is to describe the course of speaking in such a way as to affirm its control by the very objects it describes rather than by 'influences external to these objects'. External influences are everything other than the object.

To do such an affirmation in speech is to create the speech as the kind of copy whose production is independent of the commitment of the speaker to any particular outcome. The speaker must demonstrate that his commitment to the outcome as a product supersedes (and makes irrelevant) his commitment to any particular substantive outcome. He must show his commitment to the product by making it the kind of thing that 'appears' free from commitment. The inability to show this is talked about as bias, favouritism, interest, ideology. He must show commitment to non-commitment and this commitment is unquestionable.

One who truly shows commitment to non-commitment—the

creator of objective speech—is one who shows that his very speech as it is accomplished surveys, detects, and eliminates all the interested residues of commitment that could be influential.

We have tried to show how the idea of bias can be used (by us) to point to the uneasiness of a social scientific 'culture' that transforms speech into a thing, inasmuch as this very transformation converts the one who speaks into the same kind of thing as he speaks about. We have called such a programme 'positivism' and we have tried to make the life which supports it more transparent through our example.

This life as disclosed through our speech makes reference to a version of what is 'internal' and 'external' to speech, to the difference between 'private' and 'public', to a conception of self and of its nature, to the status of things and of external nature, to an ideal of scientific *mimesis* and to a community of co-speakers.

In disclosing these supports we have tried to follow a path laid down by Socrates: we have taken some talk (bias speech) and have shown some consequences, and some requirements for the talk as we understand them. Thus, the example affirms our version of understanding in that this could be seen in the manner in which we speak about them. We have sought to show how the requirements which we have located through their talk (and for their talk) are out of tune with whatever their talk recommends. This then led us to pose the question of what kind of life makes such inconsistency necessary or intelligible. In this exercise we then showed through our example a contrasting life (an alternative conception of speech) which enabled our analysis of their usage. In this way, the attention of others is re-directed from a concern with the facts and details to which their talk is oriented—the question of practical decisions and constraints—to a concern with the commitments underlying all speech and with their rational and moral status. We have tried to make the commitment underlying bias speech show itself intelligibly as a concern to protect this very question (the question of commitment) from being explored. In this sense, we have asked whether such a life is worth living, whether such a world is worth our commitment, and we have brought an alternative world to view.

F

4 EVALUATION

We take the situation of rejecting papers submitted to a scientific journal as an occasion for interrogating the idea of evaluation in science. We shall be concerned with (1) the methods in terms of which science treats evaluation as a problem, and (2) the grounds through which that treatment itself becomes intelligible as a move within science as a whole form of life (and by implication, the contrast between that kind of life and the world that enables our analysis).

Evaluative situations, of course, offer us an opportunity to understand the conditions and possibilities of moral action. Accepting and rejecting the work of others could be thought to provide us with information about the work evaluated, in which case acceptance or rejection would have the status of a description. But it is only the positivist form of life which furnishes such an interpretation, and in which a rejection is either (a) a description of the object of evaluation, or (b) a description of the methods through which the evaluation is generated. We hope to show, in contrast, how a rejection, in the context of positivism or any other form of life, is more like an affirmation of the law(s) of community. Rejection is a way of re-affirming the law.

It is more than coincidental that positivism provides for the intelligibility of evaluation through the development of a descriptive 'science' of evaluation, whether for ethics or aesthetics, or morals, or scientific decision making. It is central to the interests of positivism for it to require that positivist method be reflexively applicable to itself in order to decide the questions which it raises for itself. Positivism must either treat its evaluative (moral) problems as descriptive problems (see the moral philosophers and the philosophers of science), or abandon evaluation altogether as being beyond the bounds of positivist rationality. Since the latter option would bring its entire enterprise into question, positivism regularly seeks to demonstrate how its very method can solve the problem of evaluation by converting the issue into another descriptive topic.

Positivism seeks to transform an essentially moral action into a descriptive problem by recommending the 'natural' character of evaluation. 'Natural' is intended as follows: evaluation occurs by nature in the sense that it is designed to be an action that imitates the nature of that which is being evaluated; such imitation co-responds to the object of evaluation by answering to it and by reproducing it. The thinking that culminates in scientific evaluation is natural thinking in the sense that it imitates a nature and is consequently faithful to the nature which it imitates.

The development of a science of evaluation is an attempt to disguise the conventional and problematic character of evaluation behind a version of the 'correct form' of evaluating which is designed to enact the natural character of the process. The task of evaluation is to disguise through argument, evidence, and reason, the conventionality of the task. (Conventionality is a technical term meaning that the activity so described is contingent, or could be otherwise.) To evaluate is to make reference to standard and community by arguing for a necessary connection between object and decision of evaluation; the necessary connection makes reference to one of positivism's natural laws.

Thus, positivism is in a peculiar position with respect to evaluation. To refuse to face the problem is to admit that the law of positivism (its method) is without thought, i.e., is not grounded and consequently, that its law is conventional and could be quite different than it is, or only happens to be. Positivism must then create a category of 'sin'—of bad work—while respecting the constraint that this category cannot be produced through the literal application of its law and that the production of sin is itself beyond the scope of its project. Positivism seeks to handle this problem by 'naturalising' sin (bad work) by depicting it as a rule.

We shall begin in this paper by taking as a paradigmatic occasion of evaluation the rejection of papers sent to a scientific journal, and by using this occasion as a point of departure for addressing the grammar of evaluation.

I. THE POSSIBILITY OF EVALUATION

We developed our preliminary ideas from an inspection of the files of a leading scientific journal. The files are of papers rejected for the journal. The material in the files includes the actual letter of rejection sent to the author of the paper, sometimes earlier drafts of that letter, sometimes instructions sent from the journal's editor to the referee, sometimes informal comments from the referee to the editor and vice versa. For each paper the file also has a carbon copy of the rejected paper and a standardised list of questions which are supposed to aid the referee in doing the evaluation.

It is no news to suggest that a study of letters of rejection is a study of an evaluation system. But this simple fact does suggest something about the concerns we might address, and those we should ignore, in analysing letters of rejection. Some have pointed out that all evaluation systems face a version of the social order problem in the specific form: how is it possible that evaluations and especially negative evaluations are made to stick? To think about evaluation systems in this way is, of course, to raise the Hobbesian–Parsonian question of how it is that people accept outcomes, decisions, in this case evaluations, which seem, on the face of it, to be against their self-interest. But to raise the problem in this way is to show a very concrete and restricted interest in evaluation. First, it is to accept an understanding of rejection, and to treat the understanding as already secure by focusing upon its 'effects'. Asking whether or not, or why, a rejection is accepted is to forestall any inspection of the grammar of the idea. Furthermore, this way of putting the problem assents to the positivistic notion of rejection as a description, which is one of the very things we should examine. We cannot simply assume that the rejection is no more than a truth claim, some 'datum' to which a frustrated author is oriented and to which he must come to terms as true or false. Instead of posing the question as one of deciding what 'in fact' happens when a rejection is communicated to an author, we prefer to begin by providing for the possibility of the rejection itself. We here eschew the varieties of sociological conceptions of interaction, influence and the like, which presuppose rejection as non-problematic, as in treating the problem as the author's behavioural adaptation. The very thing of interest to us—the *possibility* of rejection, its intelligibility—is swept away in the behavioural version which considers evaluation as equivalent to the member's problem of disagreement. In the latter context, to reject would mean 'to disagree', and the concrete investigation would consist of an inquiry into the conditions under which authors come to accept (agree with) others' disagreements (rejections) of their work. However, to treat rejection as disagreement is, as we have said, to presuppose the intelligible character of the decision to reject. To think of this as disagreement or denial seriously misrepresents the quality of rejection in the same way that agreement misrepresents the idea of acceptance. It blocks inquiry by encouraging us to act upon the rejection by treating it as self-evident rather than to examine it as a conventional expression of its deep auspices, namely as a grammatical expression of the community's fundamental and therefore morally required form of life. The question, then, is not 'Why does an author come to agree with a rejection?' in the context of assent and denial, but rather 'How can a rejection be understood?' by way of locating the authoritative, communal conditions of knowing which serve to provide for the common intelligibility of a rejection.

II. THE RELEVANCE OF REASONS IN SCIENTIFIC EVALUATION

Positivism—exemplified in our case by the foreshortened social order problem—requires of itself that it treat evaluation as a mystery. The mystery resides in the notion that 'to evaluate' is to make an opinion for which the securing of agreement is problematic. In doing this the decisive character of evaluation is shifted from how it can possibly be understood (its status as knowledge) to how it comes to be accepted (its status as opinion). The *problem* of evaluation is in this view one of formulating the conditions for its acceptance (how do men become persuaded?) rather than of formulating the conditions under which it first becomes possible as an intelligible idea (how do men come to know?). The following is a referee's comment that can be thought to be his reason for rejecting the paper: 'This paper is not new'.

Because the evaluations of science are accompanied by reasons, the persuasive character of evaluation tends to be located in the reason (the paper deserves rejection because it is not new). It is assumed, accordingly, that it is the reason which induces men to accept the evaluation, i.e., the existence of a reason makes him accept the opinion that the paper should be rejected. But the identity or intelligibility of the remark 'This paper is not new' depends first upon seeing that it *is* a reason, whether correct or incorrect, fair or unfair. Whether it is persuasive or not depends upon its being an intelligible reason; in order to address its correctness one must first understand that a reason exists and can be assessed according to its correctness, which is the contingent which generates agreement and disagreement. Seeing newness *as* a reason, in other words, presupposes a grasp of what *could* be a reason in the first place.

We now want to show how reasons cannot provide an analytic formulation for the acceptance of an opinion because the indexicality of opinions renders any actual reason defeasible (defeatable), thus divesting it of the analytic requirement that it will certainly persuade. This in itself is no news, for the idea has been regularly available in ordinary language philosophy. Consequently, our principal concern is to demonstrate not merely the defeasibility of reasons, but the fact that reasons are themselves glosses to the question 'How does evaluation become intelligible?' They are a gloss, not because any reason will do, but because any reason is only a surface description (or showing) of the deeper authority in terms of which any reason becomes an intelligible reason. Reason cannot give evaluation its grounded analytic status because reasons only become intelligible in terms of authoritative auspices which prefigure and ground the possibility of reasons.

For example, two contrasting systems of evaluation are depicted by the metaphors power and science. Imagine an evaluation system where a solution turns completely on what sociologists call power, where what the referee says holds automatically. In such a system an adequate letter of rejection would involve just one word: No. As sociologists we can expect that such a system will be backed by some form of force and that the reject will have no choice but to accept the rules of the system. Rejects in this system have virtually no resources for challenging unfavourable decisions. Rather than asking how authors can possibly accept referee judgements, we might wonder how on earth they can possibly not accept them. The only resource the power system gives authors is the question: 'Is so-and-so the referee?' If he is and he says no, then his decision stands and that is it. Imagine (true example) an applicant for a teaching position who received the following rejection:

Dear Sir:
     We regret to inform you that your application for a post as lecturer at ——— University has been unsuccessful.

This kind of example raises the further question of how we can even provide for the intelligibility of this speech as a rejection. Like it, many rejections in everyday life raise such problems in the sense that by merely describing themselves as rejections they satisfy whatever conditions of evaluation their users accept and accredit. However, science does not operate like this.

Let us note a first attribute of 'Scientific Journal'[1] rejections: they are all supposed to have reasons. This rather obvious point can be demonstrated by the fact that rejected authors can criticise letters of rejection which omit reasons. For example, one author writes to the editor of the journal:

It is a hard pill to swallow for people to say they don't agree with you without stating a single specific reason . . .

[1] This is a cover name for the actual journal studied, which is a major one in the natural sciences.

Another author writes:

> To have one's work criticised unfairly by an unknown critic is bad enough, but not to know the criticisms and hence to be utterly powerless to offer any kind of defense in any matter whatsoever [is even worse].

It is fair to say that every 'Scientific Journal' rejection is seen by authors as having a reason or else as being deficient because it does not have one. However, the important question concerns the character of reasons as solutions to the analytic problem of evaluation. In other words, does the notion of reason(s) capture the analytic character of scientific evaluation?

The following suggest some of the possible reasons, i.e., adequate reasons, which referees are encouraged to treat as maxims.

Along with the paper they are to evaluate, all referees are sent a standardised list of questions, the gist of which is: 'Is it new?' 'Is it correct?' 'Is it important?' Now of course, just this list is not enough. Referees must know some rules for assessing the correspondence of the questions on the list to the object of evaluation, for distinguishing the new from the not new, the important from the unimportant. Learning these correspondence rules could be one meaning of scientific socialisation. Scientific referees would operate much in the way that coders operate. The list of questions would be their coding instructions.[2]

There are several ways to demonstrate that referees do not, and sometimes could not, produce adequate rejections just by using the formal instructions about newness, importance, and correctness. In deciding whether to accept or reject a paper, referees concern themselves not only with newness, importance, and correctness, but also with the practical consequences of their decision. Two private notes from referees to editors:

> I see no justification for giving the authors an opening wedge for additional papers that will be just as murky.

> Perhaps in view of the publication of his earlier paper to

[2] For the coding metaphor as a description of the ways calculi fail to reproduce behaviour, see Harold Garfinkel, *Studies in Ethnomethodology*, New York: Prentice-Hall, 1967, pp. 18–24.

which this is a sequel . . . and because of ——'s prestige in [science], this paper should be given space in the SJ.

More interestingly, whether the paper is seen as important enough can vary with the consequences of the decision, i.e., some papers do not have to be as important as others to be accepted:

> While we like to encourage foreign authors to send us brief reports of research which they subsequently publish in greater detail in their own journals, we are wondering whether the importance of the work in these cases is such as to warrant our publishing [them].

It is not that the mere existence of the formal criterion of importance determines the acceptability of the paper, but that importance itself turns on the variety of practical circumstances which attend each particular paper.

Sometimes the referee can make a decision before he has successfully applied the coding instructions:

> It seems to me that if it [the paper] needs squelching (which I strongly suspect) then it needs a fairly thorough job of picking out not just one weak point but quite a few. I don't feel up to spending the time required to acquire the erudition needed to do a really good job.

What leads to this decision? Clearly not a careful application of some formal criteria.

The reverse is also true. Decisions can remain up in the air after the formal instructions have been carefully followed:

> However I have no objection if you want to publish it. If you want to reject it, I furnish a letter below.

Sometimes the referees do not see the coding instructions as applicable to a paper. That is to say, they cannot assess the newness, importance, and correctness of a paper. When this happens, it is not necessarily true that the fate of the paper is seen as undecidable; rather, whatever it might be (other than newness, etc.) that the referees see as grounds for a decision can be taken as 'enough' to decide.

Referees can, if you like, 'invent' new grounds for rejection. This fact is not surprising to those of us who have observed people making decisions, but consider this phenomenon in the light of the coding instruction model of rejection. It is just not true that referees are limited by the official list of questions they are presented with. Just the opposite. Good refereeing involves making decisions anyway when the formal instructions do not quite fit.

The idea that reason decisively locates the character of evaluation is to see reasons as doing persuasion. On the other hand, we are suggesting that while reasons can and do persuade, this 'effect' does not capture their analytic status because such a status is acquired through the notion of how a reason reflexively performs a demonstration of the authority in terms of which it is grounded. We do not ask what reasons do, and then answer that they persuade. Rather, we want to know how it is that reasons *can* persuade.

Thus, while it might be true that science differs from other forms of evaluation in its preoccupation with reasons, it is wrong to locate this preoccupation as the decisive feature of scientific evaluation. The preoccupation with reasons is itself licensed by a conception of evaluation 'as having to be backed by a reason'. It is then not the reason *per se*, but the idea of the requiredness of a reason which gives scientific evaluation its distinctive character. To be preoccupied with having to give a reason is to display a concern for the grounds of evaluation; in this sense, it is fair to say of scientific evaluation that it shows a concern with the grounds of evaluation—with its possibility—that other forms do not show, and that such a concern is demonstrated through the use of reason. But, and this is a fundamental qualification, the reason does not constitute the feature, it displays the feature by making reference to the concern which provides for it. Thus, rationality is ascribed (by us) not on the basis of whether a 'reason' is present, but in terms of the ground for the demand that it be present.

So we do say that scientific evaluation distinguishes itself from other forms by its reflexivity, i.e., by its concern to understand itself. However, this kind of reflexivity is most concrete and circumscribed, for what it amounts to is the effort to formulate itself (to describe itself) under the auspices of the selfsame interests in terms of which it chooses to describe every matter. This is not only troublesome, but impossible, since nothing can be both a topic and resource at the same time and still remain wholly 'descriptive'.

Scientific reflexivity is then a form of concrete self description. It produces reasons in order to display its concrete interest in the possibility of evaluation by treating such a possibility as the empirical problem of *how an evaluation is actually decided* rather than as a method of making reference to the authoritative canon in terms of which that evaluation is sanctioned. In other words, scientific reflexivity avoids the grammatic problem: the problem of its own intelligible and sanctionable grounds of community.

Evaluation in the grammatic sense is then a problem of self reference, rather than its concrete presentation, in that to evaluate is to formulate how one can evaluate. This understanding is destroyed when we limit our conception of such self reference to the giving of reasons. To display self through evaluation is instead to make reference to the authoritativeness of a community in terms of which the performance of self becomes intelligible. Thus, evaluation must first settle the question of itself—of how it (evaluation) is to be understood— where this 'how' makes reference not to the way it is done, but to the auspices under which it is done.

A formulation of evaluation which merely describes its doing— how it is used—is concrete because it glosses the understanding that any usage acquires its authority in terms of auspices which are 'deeper' than the usage, a point we shall not examine.

III. REASONS AS RULES

Reasons come to acquire their authority as solutions to the scientific problem of evaluation when they are converted into rules. Reasons become rules when they can be reformulated as adequate maxims for the production of the evaluation. The notion of rules then serves to provide an orderly character to the evaluation process by reconstructing the decision (e.g., a rejection) as an orderly process, the requiredness of which is controlled by the work being evaluated. Given the understanding of 'rule' as the nature that governs, the transformation of reasons into rules is a method of showing that an evaluation is determined by the *nature* of that upon which it acts. This nature is supposed to be the decisive and relevant character of the work and consequently, to make a reason a rule is to say that one's evalaution is ruled by that which is decisive to the work (rather than caprice, interest, 'external' conditions, or 'irrelevant' features). To present rules for evaluation is to display oneself as ruled by that which is relevant, i.e., as ruled by the work as the relevance.

Seen in this way, rules can never appear as solutions to the problem of describing the possibility of evaluation, for rule is itself a construction which is grounded in a decision which licenses as authoritative one particular way of showing oneself as ruled by the nature of the work. Rule in this sense is a method of displaying one's responsibility rather than a description of one's practice; it only becomes intelligible as a description of practice against this tacit background of responsibility and authority.

There is another sense in which the sociological meaning of what it is to follow these rules is problematic. As we have said, the formal instructions are presented to referees in a series of standardised questions. The problem is that just answering these questions can never make for an adequate rejection. Basically, this is because adequate rejections must contain *decisions*, yet answers to the questions do not provide in any natural way for a decision. For example, there is the simple fact that referees sometimes cannot give yes-or-no answers to the questions. When asked, 'Does the article contain sufficient new results. . .?' some referees answer, 'Probably, but debatable', 'Yes—but marginal', 'I doubt it'. In other words, the connection between rule ('Is it new?', etc.) and decision (accepting or rejecting the paper) is contingent and, consequently, decision cannot be entailed by rules. Thus rule does not formulate a solution to decision but is more like the *ad hoc* reconstruction of the concrete practice of following the rule.

It gets more complex when we consider the whole set of questions at once. One referee answers the editor's query as to whether the results are new: 'Yes, if they are right.' Another:

> If the derivation is correct, or even contains elements of correctness, then the result is important enough to deserve prompt publication.

This referee adjusts his standards of correctness to allow for the paper's importance. The first referee will not evaluate newness until he has determined correctness. So, perhaps very new, papers need not be as correct as less new, very correct need not be as important as less correct, very important need not be as new as less important, etc., etc. Is scientific refereeing like a nightmarish multiple choice test where it is not only that there are no clear-cut answers, but to answer any one question you must also know the answer to all the others?

Even if a referee succeeds somehow in answering all of the questions, he does not have a decision. Say a paper is possibly correct, relatively new, and more or less unimportant, is it to be rejected or not?

The weight of all of these points makes it fair to say that we can never reproduce a referee's decision just by knowing the official standards or rules by which he made his decision. In other words, even if the sociologist of science spends years learning to distinguish scientific newness from oldness, importance from unimportance, correctness from incorrectness, he can still never reproduce a scientific referee's decision.

We are beginning, with this point, to suggest how complex refereeing is in relation to the idea of rules. It is not as if the rules for the act stand to the act as method stands to outcome. Referees use their rules very differently. Consider these comments by referees about the job they must do:

> This by no means exhausts my detailed criticisms but I will not burden you with the rest of them unless you feel the objection raised in the first paragraph is not conclusive.

> However, I have no objection if you want to publish it. If you want to reject, I furnish a letter below.

> I don't feel up to spending the time required to acquire the erudition needed to do a really good job [of squelching].

> To increase the chance of remaining anonymous, I have written these various reports as though they would have been from different referees, although this has never been stated. It is my wish that nothing be written to the authors indicating the number of referees involved.

All of these comments clearly demonstrate that adequate scientific refereeing requires that referees organise their letters of rejection so as to produce a result—a rejection, or better, a good argument for rejection.

Where do rules fit into this model of rejection? It is not that rules give referees a method for producing a rejection. It is that given a referee wants to do a rejection, he attends to the rules or instructions on how to produce the effect he wants. It is something like a logician who wants to do a formal proof. The rules of logic do not provide a correct answer, they provide a guide to how answers should be defended. Reasons should be seen in a similar way. The reasons in a rejection are neither the method by which the decision was made nor a description of everything that is true of a paper; reasons are a defence of, an argument for, a decision. This is to say that reasons neither describe the rejected paper (its characteristics), nor the method of their production, but serve the referee as a set of concrete grounds and defences for organising this particular affirmation of some communal version of adequate work. Given that a rejection is required, rules are ways of showing the rejection and its requiredness. It is not that the rules provide a correct answer, but that they provide a rationale for any actual answer so as to make it intelligible and thus defensible as an answer.

IV. GRAMMAR

One version of a referee's problem is (a) concrete: how his argument can generate agreement; (b) analytical: how simply by arguing he shuts off argument (rebuttal). Another version would be that the concrete problem is one of shutting off argument and the analytic one a matter of putting himself (his rejection) in a scientific form of life such that an oriented author would see him there and in so doing accept the rejection. Either version requires certain notions of justice, democracy, dispute, community, etc., if we are to provide the grounds which make referees' reasons intelligible to authors as rejections. We must formulate argument as it displays various just or democratic auspices and thus intelligibly grounds the reason. Giving a reason is how 'agreement' is produced, actually how acceptance is produced even when called agreement. It is how rebuttal, disagreement, etc., are shut off. It is the grammar: give a reason and you produce acceptance. Giving a reason is not at all the same thing as distinguishing reasons which produce agreement and those which do not. What we suggest here is that the author has to see that a reason has been offered, not that he must agree.

To give a reason as grammar can be connected to science as a form of life because it is to make the decision just. The author as the referee's analytic construction will accept a just decision because of the scientific form of community. There may be cranky or wrong-headed authors and so on but they are not provided for in forms of life except as concretely irritating irrelevancies. Referees are not casting directors, monarchs, lovers—'power' is not their game—and in this regard their decisions are defeasible in ways decisions by the others cannot be. No one looks to casting directors, etc., for the kind of democratic justice which serves science. Lovers can leave one another simply because they choose to, and still be called lovers. Referees cannot reject papers simply because they choose to and still be called referees.

Now the interesting thing is that reasons, as justice, do not require detailed substantive agreement by the author in order to shut off rebuttal, in order to be accepted by him. Agreement in this substantive sense is not produced by a reason (doesn't need to be produced). If we want to think of rejections as arguments, they can take two forms *vis-à-vis* the recipient or author: (1) The argument is followable as an argument, which is different from (2) Do you agree with the argument? Letters of rejection require (1) (a reason is followable if it has the status of a reason), but not (2). That is, rejections and reasons are not established in the form of life as, say, 'findings', so their status does not depend on consensus (perhaps this is why editors do not need consensus or even a favourable majority to publish some papers).

That the argument is followable means that it is anyman's argument. Which is to say that, contrary to monarchies, scientific rejections are deliberated. The just decision is deliberated in so far as *the referee is anyman since the author claims to be speaking to anyman*. No idiosyncrasy, no secrets, no mere incompatibility or whim corresponds to anyman. Seen this way, the 'extra scientific' factors proposed by empiricists as the methods of referees and editors are anything but irrational.[3]

[3] That there could be an 'extra scientific' factor is probably impossible. The term is a normalising metaphor for departures from science, but departures which can only be seen as instances of that selfsame science.

Another aspect of argument as shutting off rebuttal without doing so monarchically: since scientific decisions are disputable they can only be disputed in the concrete by recognising that they *are* arguments and therefore contingent. It shuts off argument by reminding the author that any argument could be interminable and thus never produce a resolution. Furthermore, the argument form permits the referee to *claim*, and claim explicitly, that although he is a person he has the vision of anyman (the scientific community) and thus transcends his concrete being. That he is just, dissolves his status as concrete person and makes the decision sound. These are characteristic of the argument form itself, and do not depend on the contingency that agreement will be produced in the author. The reason is the rational scientific virtue. It is the rule in the sense that it needs only to be seen as having been offered, not assessed.

Another way of saying this is that in writing his scientific paper the author claims to be interchangeable with the community and its representative, the referee. He claims to have seen what anyman could see, and to be reporting this to anyman, from one mouthpiece to another. This claim is what is rejected. If reason is the rule, the giving of a reason serves both to indicate that interchangeability had been available to the author and to assign the failure of interchangeability elsewhere than the one giving the reason. In this way it also excludes the one (author) from the many (scientists), of course. Perhaps it is the task of the referee in providing a reason to show the author that the latter has not conformed to the interchangeability rule. The referee, as anyman, cannot see himself also as the author (for whatever substantive grounds) and thus the author has (concretely?) failed to make them interchangeable. A rejected author is not speaking to anyman, he is not the mouthpiece of nature, and thus referee as anyman cannot locate himself in the scheme offered by the author (there is no place in it for anyman and so it cannot be science). The deep source of authority here is the exact opposite of the source for monarchy in that the form of life to which the author is committed is not personal and cannot be personified, and thus for the referee to show that he is not personifying is enough to make acceptable to the author the rejection of his claim. The form of life cannot be personified by the referee, it can only be represented by him. Monarchies, on the other hand, serve to shut off debate either through the achievement of concrete consensus or by declaration, the latter especially being a resource attached to the person. Thus the fool as conscience—the one who argues with the monarch at great risk—is a necessary feature of those forms of life, and the opposite of science. The fool and his monarch argue to agree or not, not to provide reasons. Clearly, for example, a fool could not be anonymous. A referee can be anonymous precisely because he speaks for anyman as the recipient of another's claim to be nature's messenger, within the interchangeable community of nature's public. The fool is one who seems not to 'hear' the declaration. The author, because the referee adopts the argument format itself, cannot help but hear the reason.

Notice too that in science a rebuttal to rejection is not accomplished (except perhaps privately, and therefore irrelevantly in our terms) by having the author explain how the referee came to give the reason he did. *That* the referee is just (shown by giving a reason) is not offset by *explaining* how he came to do so or how he gave the reason he did. Science is not politics, in which an explanation would turn a reason into ideology or some such thing, because it involves collecting (everybody an anyman) rather than segregating (choosing among varieties of everyman).[4] This is to say that in the one case, showing there are grounds for a decision is adequate; whereas in the political case there are 'better' grounds than others, which means in politics his reasons are *his*; in science, his reasons are, if adequate, *anyman's*. To 'explain' a reason is in the political sense to differentiate its source and thus segregate it from its other possible sources. It is a tactic which is unavailable in collecting forms of life. (Think of families here, families of all sorts and forms.)

It is then misleading to say that authors accept rejections, for they do not treat rejections as 'proofs'; a rejection is not an action with which one agrees, but is rather an action one understands. Authors accept rejections by understanding

---

[4] Naturally, scientific work can be made political, and this is precisely what occurs when scientific decisions get explained in terms of, say, the social interests of the deciders. And these explanations can be eminently sensible ones. But we are then dealing analytically with politicisation and not science.

G

them, and the analytic character of rejection is provided for by showing how it is organised as an intelligible expression of the community to which both referee and author profess membership. Again, rejections are not descriptions, explanations or proofs, but methods of making reference to the authority of community. Yet it is in the interests of a positivistic culture to treat rejection as a matter of description, explanation, and/or proof, because it is only in this way that rejection (and evaluation) can become another descriptive topic for positivistic method.

V. POSITIVIST FORM OF LIFE

The attempt to organise evaluation through a descriptive procedure is a move in a positivist game. Here any and every evaluation is transformed in order to demonstrate its character as a descriptive reproduction of nature. Evaluation is purported to 'reflect' objective, discernible 'properties' of the author's paper, whereby the referee's concrete act of producing a thoughtful decision is treated as an imitation of the nature of the paper, given the understanding that both paper and decision were constructed to follow the source of nature. Rules for evaluating are then designed to reproduce anyman's response to the paper by controlling for the operation of extraneous influences—will, value, subjectivity—which could intervene between the referee's thought as anyman and the thing that is the paper. Rules of evaluation are designed to join thought and things by forcing the referee to submit to a method which, if followed, guarantees the reproduction of things through thought.

The reason supplied by the referee is his procedure for reconstructing his decision as a natural course of action which was controlled by the paper; the paper functions as a constraint to which the referee's decision is assumed to be responsive, as a reproduction of the essential character of the paper. The reason then, has to demonstrate its character as the grounds of thought of anyman reading the paper and thus, the reason seeks to join the referee's decision to the paper by demonstrating the requiredness of the decision as an essential feature of the paper.

To say that the decision is 'necessary' according to the

descriptive mode of evaluation is to assert that the idea of the paper provides for—as one of its essential possibilities—the referee's decision. In a sense, the decision is internal to, or required by, the paper as one of its (the paper's) essential parameters. The decision 'belongs' to the paper in that it is a version of what anyman *must* make out of the paper because the nature of the paper is such as to permit this and only this possibility. The reason then, must argue for the decision's belonging to the paper by nature (and not by convention) and thus, the reason must argue for its requiredness. One format for demonstrating such requiredness is the calculus of rules which is designed to typify a course of evaluative action that is natural rather than conventional. The fact that such formats are nevertheless defeasible and conventional, as we have tried to show, recommends to the sociologist the linguistic and grammatic rather than descriptive character of the rules.

To recapitulate at this point. There are two typical ways in which reasons are used within the positivistic form of life: each use of reason suggests a different descriptive possibility which positivism assigns to the evaluation process. In one case, rejection means something like 'bad'—a condemnation—and the decision to reject is treated as if it were a description of a bad work. In this case, acceptance and rejection become descriptions respectively of what constitutes praiseworthy and inadequate works and the reason is treated as a description of such usage. In such a case, the reasons are organised around various surface criteria of the work and these criteria become formulable as 'indicators' of a bad or good work. However, such a treatment opens itself to two large problems: when properties of the work are treated as criteria they function somewhat like 'causes' of the decision, yet we saw that it is impossible to construct a necessary and sufficient list of such causes from criteria because in each and every case the status of a criterion as a cause glosses the vast amount of interpretive work in which the referee engages to normalise, standardise, and assimilate his extra-criterial knowledge to the conditions of such a correct form model.

But the essential point here is that the use of 'bad' is a moral idea,[5] and not descriptive in the sense that it is different in

[5] J. Kovesi, *Moral Notions*, London: Routledge & Kegan Paul, 1967.

kind rather than degree from 'yellow' and 'table'. And even if this is denied there is the further problem that an analytic formulation of 'bad' is obliterated when we treat its usage as the thing to be reproduced, for this amounts to saying that the moral ground of 'bad' is the equivalent of how it is used, and not even positivists could mean this. To formulate 'bad' as a description of professional usage is to circumvent the authoritativeness of inquiry in which such usage has to be grounded. It is to treat the deep problem of 'bad' as a matter that is transrational and beyond communal control and thus, it is to exempt one's very grounds from inquiry.

This is all by way of saying that even the notion of a 'bad' work fails to capture the sense of rejection, in that the doing of rejection is more than saying, using, or applying 'bad' whether in terms of explicit or tacit 'criteria': the use of bad is only a surface feature of rejection in that such a use makes reference to and brings to bear an entire tradition of authority of which the usage is only a limp expression. To paraphrase Nietzsche, 'bad' is a manifestation of the will to power which its use conceals and covers over.

The second positivist option for treating evaluation is closely related. Besides treating the rejection as a description of a paper, the giving of reasons for a rejection can also be a way of offering an 'explanation' for one's decision. The reason becomes ego's account of how he decided, and since the account should be grounded in the work itself, the reason is designed to display the course of action of reading the work. The reason is then treated as the referee's self report, his description of the activity of reading-to-a-decision and as such it is supposed to guarantee that the reading was controlled only by the constraint of the work. Yet a rejection cannot stand as a referee's description of self, for to describe self thus would be to use as unanalysed resources the very work being evaluated.

This is to say that one does not address the grammar of rejection by 'explaining' how he produced the action for this is a concrete solution to an analytic problem. This is a conventional variant of the usage solution which again skirts the analytic problem of rejection. This solution stands to the first as say, Descartes stands to Ryle. Even if one succeeds in producing such an 'explanation' one can only do so under the auspices of an authoritative version of knowledge which the explanation itself cannot address. Reasons as explanations are only rationalisations for an unanalysed authority in terms of which a referee is acting, although when they are displayed they appear as naturalistic descriptions of rejection as produced by self as anyman; but these displays, as we have seen, also depend upon a morality in terms of which such an anyman becomes intelligible: in this case a positivist form of life.

To say that positivism treats evaluation like description is to say that it treats evaluation as other than it is. What is decisive about evaluation is that it cannot be described in a way that is free from an evaluative context; evaluation is only intelligible as an instance of the selfsame idea which it purports to describe. Deeply then, evaluation cannot be description, for it is a method of affirming a way to evaluate and its disguise of such a proposal in a descriptive format only conceals the fact that evaluation performs a recommendation for its own intelligible character.

The question then is not 'why evaluation?', but 'why does science require itself to transform its moral judgments into descriptive statements?' Granted that behind every practice lies a concealed morality that animates the practice,[6] why does a practice like science treat its morality as if it were a matter to be described? Why does science lie?

If science did not lie it would have to concede that the grounds of its authority cannot be addressed by its method, that its reason for being is beyond the scope of its project, that it cannot be reflexively self-critical. Science would have to admit either that it does not know why it does as it does, or that it does what it has always done, or that it has no good reason for doing what it does aside from the effects or consequences of its doing. Science would have to admit that there is no reason internal to science for rationally grounding what it does.

In treating evaluation as description, science makes the claim that its reason for doing as it does is no different from any other matter it studies and that this reason is a descriptive topic for science. The need for evaluation is the need for a Law which is itself beyond the law; it is the desire to create a law which is

6 Nietzsche, *The Twilight of the Idols*, Baltimore and Harmondsworth: Penguin, 1968.

itself not part of the field of application for the operation of the selfsame law.

ADDENDUM

After a public presentation of *Evaluation* the editor of a 'scientific' journal in England invited us to submit it for publication. We did so, on the assumption that, even if the editor had second thoughts, its capacity to elicit rejections would further exemplify our argument. This is just what happened. We reproduce the following three evaluations of the referees as such an example. Each evaluation, lettered A, B, and C, is followed by our response.

EVALUATION A

This paper is philosophy, not sociology or history of science. Properly speaking, it should be reviewed by a philosopher of science. The argument is interesting and controversial but, as a sociologist, I find that it is unconvincing, highly selective, and repetitious. No attempt is made to relate the discussion to relevant literature on the sociology and history of science, such as Kuhn's work on paradigms and recent work on evaluation by scientific journals (e.g., Zuckerman and Merton, *Minerva*, 1971). The 'data' which the authors provide is insufficient to substantiate their thesis. The nature of the 'sample' from which the 'data' is drawn is not specified (i.e., period of time covered by the file of correspondence, number of articles reviewed and rejected). In addition, the journal described is very probably —— —— (judging from the former institutional affiliations of two of the authors and from the fact that Merton and Zuckerman, who are also at Columbia, have published an analysis of the files of this journal). If this is the case, it is misleading to omit the fact that this journal accepts over 80% of all articles submitted to it (Zuckerman and Merton, *op. cit.*). Rejection is the exception, not the rule. Therefore it is not true, as stated on page 15 [see p. 87 above], that the sociologist of science could not reproduce the referee's decisions. He could in the majority of cases. Evidently the authors had such a small supply of quotations which 'support' their case that they use two of them twice (pages 10 and 15 [see pp. 83, 87 above]). Finally, terms like 'form of life' are not standard sociological terms and are not defined by the authors.

The problem of the evaluation of scientific work by scientific journals is a very interesting one but this paper is too narrow in its approach to be a satisfactory contribution to such an analysis.

RESPONSE TO A

This referee first seeks to exempt himself from responsibility for his evaluation through distinctions between the disciplines of sociology, philosophy, and history of science, distinctions which he nevertheless leaves unexplored. So, he first shows an authoritative but unformulated notion of the legitimate limits and boundaries of discussion. The limit is not that beyond which nothing can be said, it seems, since the referee does speak beyond the limit by going ahead and reviewing the paper even though it is beyond the limit. The limit, apparently, is that which one cannot impersonate, in the sense that one can only impersonate that which is securely internal. The idea of disciplines prepares us to internalise and externalise, to discriminate speech which impersonates as within the limit and other speech as outside the limit. The internal, then, is not that which is brought in from outside but that which is already inside and thus already secure; similarly, the external is that which is already securely outside. These distinctions allow referee A both to reject the paper as being outside of sociology and to repudiate his role in the rejection, for in the eventuality of conflict between referees he can claim 'after all' to be a sociologist and thus unable to impersonate the philosophy he takes the paper to be.

The fact that he finds the argument 'interesting' could be contrasted with the 'unconvincing' character of the paper which he identifies 'as a sociologist', leading us to wonder what capacity of his life his version of its interesting character represents. In this regard he raises one problem of evaluation we noted in the paper, namely to invoke the disparate criteria of newness (interest) and correctness (conviction).

He has an idea that speech should be related to previous

discussions (the relevant literature) which permits him to avoid seeing the historic discussion in which the paper participates as a discussion at all. So again, he has an authoritative version of what it is to relate to one's tradition, namely to the literature that is the speech which has preceded present speech. That all this speech makes reference to a language of moral affirmation as a grounding of these particular speeches, whatever their chronology, is apparently not the kind of thing he means by 'relevance'.

This referee has notions of 'data', of 'substantiating the thesis' through certain kinds of procedures which he leaves unquestioned. These rules specify not only sampling operations, but a descriptivist requirement that the paper re-produce 'what is the case', i.e., he sees the *analysis* of rejection as a *description* of the regularity of rejection.

Further, because of this rule he is led to assume that the frequency of rejection means that a scientist could 'reproduce the referee's decisions'. Here then, is a concrete notion of 'reproducing' as enumerating or 'accounting for' concrete occasions, rather than as a laying out of grounds which would make such enumeration possible. In all of this we see the operation of an authoritative set of auspices which sanction his conception of adequate speaking: adequate speech is speech which imitates the speech which is one's subject. Just as positivist evaluation is expected to imitate the paper being evaluated, the speech that is the paper is expected to enumerate the speech which is the paper's topic.

We repeat that our interest is not in refuting this referee but in pointing to the 'form of life' which makes him possible. Consequently, when he asks for a 'definition' of form of life, we might remind him of the authoritative auspices which provide for the intelligibility of his own evaluation: auspices organised in a central way around notions of adequate (rational) speech as speech which preserves ordinary understanding through a version of description that assumes the identity of the words one uses with the matters those words address. Rather than an analysis of how this identity is possible, we are constrained in positivism to produce the identity by treating the achievement as exterior to the production.

EVALUATION B

This is an appalling example of a hideous genre: American sociologese. It's apparently an extract from a forthcoming book and in that context it might begin to make sense, though I doubt it. As it stands, it's almost unintelligible. It *seems* to be arguing that evaluation in science is 'grounded' in communal authority, and that its nature can't be adequately understood in purely descriptive terms, i.e., positivistically, i.e., by science itself. But apart from this highly questionable identification of science with descriptivism and the positivist philosophy of science, the whole project is in various ways confused. For one thing, the authors seem to regard their problem as a 'grammatic' one, as 'analytic', as concerned with the 'possibility' or 'intelligibility' of evaluation in science, and though they signally fail to explain what they mean, these characteristics strongly suggest certain contemporary views about the non-empirical nature of *philosophical* techniques; yet the authors seem to think it necessary to give their investigation an empirical air by appealing to evidence about editorial replies sent to authors submitting papers to a scientific journal. For another thing, this whole approach to the problem of evaluation in science, though possibly original, is perverse and obscurantist, and can only be understood, I suppose, as a desperate attempt to get a specifically *sociological* angle on the problem. For the problem of evaluation in science is the problem of the kinds of considerations and criteria relevant to the appraisal and criticism of scientific theories: the problem of the acceptance and rejection of papers submitted to scientific journals is clearly not the same problem, yet nowhere do the authors try to distinguish the two and there are obvious points at which the problem they tackle breeds its own idiosyncratic confusions. For example, the difference between *accepting* the editor's rejection and agreeing with it is not noticed, belatedly, until p. 17 [see p. 88 above], and then its importance is emphasised only in manuscript, as an after thought; but despite this emendation they continue to say, inconsistently, that 'giving a reason is how "agreement" is produced . . . is how rebuttal, disagreement, etc., are shut off'. There are many other shortcomings, e.g., the tendency to suppose that all evalua-

tion is 'moral', and the astonishing suggestion that justice is simply giving some reason or other (however inadequate). But the whole paper is so full of obscurity, confusion, and bad argument that it's impossible to identify all its defects.

RESPONSE TO B

This is a more difficult evaluation to respond to because the anger shown in the referee's gratuitous comments could deflect us from concentrating upon the auspices which provide the intelligibility of the evaluation.

When he says that 'it is almost unintelligible', we see his remark as peculiar (the idea of being more or less intelligible) because what *is* intelligible to him is the unintelligibility of the paper. If unintelligible suggests (as Wittgenstein noted) that 'I cannot go on' his attempt to go on denies his thesis. That he can go on shows his descriptivism, shows how he treats unintelligibility as a thing, and we recognise this as his cry of pain. He is confronted with speech that is no-thing (not a thing) and which his form of life requires him to convert into a thing. This is how he can treat his comment on unintelligibility as small talk, moving on to show how intelligible the paper is through his subsequent comment. Actually, in seeing him understand intelligibility, we see the auspices for his entire evaluation, he has a decisive conception of speech that allows him to talk about unintelligibility intelligibly and thus to deny the concrete detail of his argument. His descriptivism concentrates in the paper the responsibility for what the paper is, exempting the reader from any participation by converting the speech he makes into speech that is made by the paper.

In his remark about our 'empirical air' this referee seems to think that we are interested in characterising positivism descriptively, whereas we are typifying a form of life which animates (for us) typical scientific talk. Such a recognition is only possible through our analysis and our interest lies not in 'identifying' science by describing it. What is important is that his differentiation of science from descriptivism, though cryptic, shows a particular notion of descriptivism. Reading through the gloss, description must come to factuality or some such thing for this referee, given that he wants to differentiate it from

100

science as a whole; this (unformulated) notion would make it possible that science can be 'more than' description, i.e., more than factual, by limiting the idea of description to the factual. But it maintains the positive tenet that facts describe and theories account. Though different than facts, theories continue to be subject to positive constraint because they must 'lead to' or be 'necessary for' description. Which is to say that the theories, deductions, hypotheses, etc., that this referee would stipulate to be not descriptive can only be informed by the descriptive interests they serve, and thus are *analytically* descriptive. In fact, that we could show his entire evaluation to express this authority of a descriptive interest which distinguishes concrete factuality from eventual descriptive outcomes suggests that he cannot free himself from the differentiation he makes (if that is his intent). While his speech shows his commitment just as our speech does, it also shows how he forgets the committed character of speech through his treatment of his talk as the only possible talk. Our talk, accordingly, is treated as if it must have started with his notion of description, and so our failure is not to have continued with his notion.

His notion of our failure 'to explain' what we mean rests on a particular version of explaining what is meant as words whhic are provided so that other words may turn on them; whereas our speech has shown what it means, that is, it is what it is. Our speech shows what it is as a re-presentation of that which grounds our words, rather than as tactical and syntactical arrangements whereby words explicate other words. To ground the words in language is to shift the burden from words-as-usage to the dialectic speech of which the words are only a display.

This referee sees an inconsistency between our (imputed) philosophical thesis and our 'appeal to evidence' because he treats our examples as if they were collected in response to *his* notion of data. This is to say that his understanding of data leads him to transform what we present as examples needing examination into a deficient instance of whatever he regards as data (that data must be empirically coercive?). For us to accept his critique would presuppose our commitment to his version of 'data' because in the absence of that his recognition of a 'problem' cannot be apparent to us.

Everything that follows his characterisation of 'what' the problem in evaluation is affirms his notion of evaluation which is the very commitment that our paper examined. His problem is that he does not see our refusal to live with his notion of evaluation as the very topic of the paper itself. Rather, he sees us as struggling to live up to the requirements of *his* formulation of the problem. For example, his conventions allow him to distinguish 'appraisal of theories' from 'evaluation of papers' as if the fact that two different objects are being considered has to make a difference (or that two different sets of reasons are given, or that two different sets of contingencies intervene). He is the type who probably would say that 'decision' on a paper is more *practical* than the appraisal of a theory while we would take this as a display of an analytic distinction to be uncovered through analysis.

As we have tried to show, this referee's conclusion that the paper is 'confused, obscure, and badly argued' makes reference to his unstated notion of a 'good, clear argument' and that very notion was the concern of our paper. His anger shows that he thinks his auspices self-evident and not contingent in any way. Otherwise he could not see us as merely failing to respect them, rather than choosing not to respect them. Because he does not treat our disrespect as the very point and idea which our paper affirms he ignores our auspices too, converting them into a degenerate version of his (which remain unquestioned). The referee appears much like the angry interlocutor in the Socratic dialogue who resists being treated dialectically through continual reification. His descriptivism shows in his treatment of the quality of our paper as something that is there-for-the-looking, and he can only do this by ignoring the achieved character of his own evaluation. Of course, this was the point of our paper, something his evaluation easily confirms.

EVALUATION C

Intelligibility

1. Grammar: what is the meaning in this paper.
   What is 'the grammar of the idea' (p. 4) [see p. 79 above].
          'the grammatic problem' (p. 12) [see p. 85 above].
   The word seems to add nothing but confusion whenever

it is used. It should be elaborated and justified—or dropped.

2. Analytic Indexicality (p. 7 ff) [see p. 80 ff above]: explanatory footnotes needed.

3. Equivalence of moral and evaluative: would we not want to say that whether Schweppes make good or bad orange juice is an evaluative but not a moral question in its normal usage? Would not calling it a moral question actually change the way people 'took' it—tend to make them wonder about other things instead of (say) taste and juiciness.

4. P. 13, para. 1, sentence 1 [see p. 86 above] :   ugh!

5. P. 14, lines 9–11 [see p. 86 above]:   I find this confusing at first due to the different senses of rule at beginning and end. Could it be reformulated?

Argument

1. The concrete discussion I like, but it is then generalised to 'science' and 'positivism' in a completely taken for granted way. Possibly the generalisation to science could be overlooked, but all the chit-chat about positivism proceeds without justification and entirely in the idiom of misleading anthropomorphic metaphor. Positivism, we learn, has 'interests' in terms of which it 'seeks' 'requires' 'transforms', etc.—even 'attempts to disguise the conventional and problematic character of evaluation', etc. Is positivism a culture? Is 'science' included in it? Are scientists assumed to be positivists? Or is it just that their institutional forms are permeated with it?

'The attempt to organise evaluation through a descriptive procedure is a move in a positivist game' (p. 21) [see p. 92 above]. Perhaps. But what of the explanation of this phenomenon in science? (p. 25) [see p. 95 above]. Certainly many of the things 'science would have to admit' otherwise, are readily acknowledged by many scientists. Of course science can be positivistic where scientists are not—but then what do the authors mean by science? The authors should make themselves fully explicit here and cease to hide behind anthropomorphic metaphors.

2. The authors proceed from showing that reasons for rejection in the official blurb are insufficient, to the claim that they can 'invent' new grounds for rejection. In the absence of evidence from the authors one suspects that referees here, like most others, pay scarcely any attention to the 'official' blurb and simply use implicit, tacitly accepted, procedures for evaluating, i.e., referees don't 'invent' new reasons they simply draw on a tacitly accepted stock of reasons already available.

   Incidentally here, as in many other places where the authors refer to tacit elements of science or the 'authoritative communal conditions of knowing' (p. 5), within science, reference to Michael Polanyi's work on the tacit dimension in science, with a note on how his usage differs from the authors', would be helpful. Many —— —— readers will be familiar with Polanyi and will tend to see the authors' comments in this area through Polanyi's framework. Furthermore, one wonders whether or not the authors owe Polanyi any acknowledgment?

3. Hypothesis—example—comment.
   There is confusion between
      how important a paper has to be to be published
   AND
      how the importance of a paper is influenced by the 'practical circumstances which attend (it)'.

4. Sections 2 and 3 draw upon the work of ordinary language philosophers very heavily. And they do so, for the most part, validly. It is correct and important to note the insufficiency or 'defeasibility' of reasons. However, they then think that it follows from this that 'any usage acquires its authority in terms of auspices which are deeper than the usage'. Assuming I understand the splendidly vague, issue-dodging, term 'auspices' closely enough, the work of Wittgenstein provides a sustained attack on this assumption. This should be noted since the authors refer to ordinary language philosophy. The *Phil. Investigations* are relevant here, but even more so the *Remarks on the Foundations of Mathematics*. Wittgenstein here tends to beat the 'ethno's' at their own game.

5. Finally a personal opinion. I don't believe in non-indexical statements, utterances or whatever. If the authors add a

footnote explaining 'indexicality', which I hope they will, could it include an example of a non-indexical statement? All the present paper, of course, is clearly indexical.

RESPONSE TO C

This referee organises his evaluation in terms of a nomenclature of headings which is designed to carry the analytic weight of his remarks. So, under 'intelligibility' he lists a set of 'problems' which come to matters of usage for which he requires clarification. For example, he says that the word 'grammar' adds 'nothing but confusion whenever it is used' thus raising the question of how confusion can be said to be added. That is he does not distinguish between the confusion that is the *aporia* and other senses he seems to find destructive. Evidently there is a notion of confusion here which despairs on those occasions when terms are not used with a certain degree of exactness. That he finds the speech confusing makes reference to some authoritative notion of clarity which we suggest is the very concrete notion of parsimonious and exact lexical explication of referee B.

With regard to orange juice, what referee C wants to do, but fails to formulate, is to persuade us of a difference between the moral and evaluative as one which rests on the occasions when evaluation is done. This reflects one point of our paper: positive rejection of a submitted paper is treated in the normal usage of science as the responsibility of the paper (as a responsibility of the occasion for evaluation). For this referee the morality of the occasion depends on the occasion that is inquired about rather than on the grounds of the inquiry. We are expected to deflect ourselves from any examination of 'normal usage' by conforming to whatever normal usage is thought to require. If the occasion is orange juice, which is trivial according to normal usage, one who conforms to normal usage would resist thinking of his activity as moral. But triviality only conceals the moral affirmation that any evaluation of good and bad displays. Because the referee and normal usage don't particularly care about good–bad orange juice, the referee claims we would resist calling the evaluation of good–bad orange juice moral. Yet any grading affirms some commitment by which we distinguish the many from the one with which we start, and that we can do this even with the trivial only confirms the potency of the moral-evaluative possibility. We can grade orange juice, students, ourselves, our work. A parameter of the grade is the commitment the grade displays. The worth of the activity—its trivial or important side—does not require an analytically different question, because any worth would display a commitment. Deciding whether something is worth evaluating, as with orange juice, is in this sense an evaluation of evaluation. Our paper, moreover, could be read as an evaluation of positive evaluation. Referee C engages in this very matter in his talk about orange juice. Perhaps he wouldn't want an evaluation of orange juice in a journal for which he referees, if he could get an evaluation of political democracy instead, but we would have to say that such a distinction could not be a distinction in terms of an analytical version of the moral.

Under the heading 'argument' he lists five troubles all of which make reference to his notion of rational inquiry. Again, the troubles he locates should be read—as we argued in our paper—not as characterisations which have a descriptive status when applied to the matter being responded to (to the paper) but as icons of an authoritative notion of adequacy which provide for the location of any trouble. His first objection proceeds from his identification of our analysis with description and so he desires more characterisation pertaining to 'science', 'positivism', etc. He questions our generalisation (our sampling?) only because he does not hear our speech as exemplary rather than as characterisational. Thus, he has an interest in our speech which is reminiscent of the 'culture and personality' interest, i.e., he wants to understand the relation between our use of science (or positivism) and the opinions of individual scientists (he wants some kind of warrant for assigning descriptive adequacy to our speech). This referee thinks that our talk about science has the status of a conventional community study or opinion survey, that we are speaking about science in the same way that sociologists might speak about Manchester, Edinburgh or Des Moines, Iowa. Of course this understanding is only possible given a particular and decisive notion of reading and understanding which he imposes upon us and to which his characterisations make reference: That what is to be understood is the matter which is spoken about rather than what the speech says about the speaker.

This referee wants us to be responsible to a popular author

whom he and his constituency have managed to understand and assimilate. Our silence towards this popular author suggests to the referee not indifference but a significant silence. To see our omission of citation to this author (or to any author) as significant presupposes the referee's formulation of a connection which for him is self-evident but unexplored. Yet the fact that we do not mention this author can be taken as a sign of our dependency upon him only if the referee has a theory which provides for the relevance of this absence as compared to any other absent citation that could also be generated. This theory must stipulate the grounds for our silence given the relevance of the particular author. In this case the grounds suggest that we evade responsibility because of our desire to be first and such a citation would show our secondary character. Thus, the invidious remark does not merely point to a convergence but serves to build upon a moral focus, and in this sense the very casual and perhaps off-hand comment on the absence of citation to this popular author shows as well as any other remark the operation of a particular conception of speech. This is to say that he treats our failure to mention the author as our problem, whereas we would say that his notion of the relevance of the author is his problem.

This referee does not understand the idea of 'important paper' as a feature of the circumstances which produce it; because of this he can accuse us of failing to distinguish between the idea of importance and 'circumstances which attend'. The fact that he *can* distinguish makes reference to an unexamined conception of adequate discourse, namely that the sense of a thing can be independent of the work by which that sense is achieved.

Here in items 3 and 4 the referee shows the way he understands Wittgenstein and it is important to see that one who reads Wittgenstein in this way could not be expected to understand our paper. He fails to see auspices as metaphor for form of life, instead talking about auspices as that 'vague, issue-dodging term'. The notion of vague, issue-dodging terms makes reference to the authoritativeness of his form of life which was the topic of our paper. This is to say that his very notion of auspices as a 'vague issue-dodging term' tells us less about auspices than it does about his notion of adequate speech and rational analysis. We would say that the referee's very speech 'dodges' the issue of *his* responsibility as a speaker in a way

107

quite different from how our failure to 'define' auspices dodges the issue. What is up for grabs here is how speech can dodge the issue and how his speech shows the very dodging of the issue which our paper was concerned to analyse. Thus, we would say of all these evaluations that they nicely dodge the issue of responsibility for speech by protecting the grounds of evaluation from being explored under the rubric of a characterisational or descriptivist interest. For this referee then, speech dodges the issue when it fails to organise itself as a calculus, whereas for us, speech dodges the issue when it attempts to create just such an organisation of speech, because any such calculus masks the achieved character of the evaluation itself. So, inadvertently his talk about dodging the issue raises the most important concern of the paper again but in a form which he fails to recognise.

The fact that he contrasts his last comment as a 'personal opinion' with what preceded it shows the strange idea of speech to which he subscribes, for his commitment has animated his entire talk up until this point and the idea that he only now will give his 'personal opinion' only reaffirms the positivist notion of a distinction between neutral and committed speech under the auspices of the illusion that committed speech is opinionated while neutral speech is free from such influence. Again, he makes reference to this commitment through his most casual remarks.

In sum, these evaluations were introduced not as specimens of error but as exemplifications of the very kind of commitment which our paper used as an occasion for analysis. We talked about that commitment in terms of the metaphor of positivism and these evaluations show nicely the kind of speech which hides its commitment on the grounds of a moral requirement to be protective because exposure threatens to dissolve speech into anarchy. In contrast to this conception of speech, our analysis intended to display commitment to exposing commitment as an alternative form of life.

5 SNUBS

Socrates introduced the analytic tactic of examining near-at-hand and mundane examples in order to fasten the mind on the essential feature of a problem which the example covers over. Yet his interlocutors invariably resisted this strategy on the grounds that they did not see the connection between the mundaneity of the examples and the idea toward which he was leading them. They did not see that the example neither described nor defined the idea, but served instead to re-route the mind so as to approach the idea in a way that was unencumbered by the conventions of ordinary formulations.

In this paper we use as exemplary what Freud called 'the refuse of the phenomenal world' in order to make reference to very important matters. ('Is it not possible . . . for very important things to betray themselves in very slight indications?')[1] The very important matter we will address is the dialectic between Self and Other and the complex of problems connected

[1] Sigmund Freud, *A General Introduction to Psychoanalysis*, New York: Permabooks, 1963, p. 31.

109

with togetherness and separateness, unity and difference. The very slight indications which we use as examples are occasions of greeting, snubbing, and rebuffing. The substance of the paper provides an exemplification of a method for getting from the mundane examples to the important matters, and in the process serves to demonstrate a conception of analysis that is neither subservient to conceptions of usage like ethnomethodology, nor unreflexive like phenomenological social psychology.

Thus, we will display, by example, a certain conception of analysis. While we begin with what could be called a criticism of another conception of analysis, the paper cannot succeed if it is only a criticism, at least as that term is conventionally used.[2] If by criticism is meant to affirm a difference, then we must do something else. Moreover, we hope our analysis will show why affirming a difference, even a superiority, is not a sufficient accomplishment.

I

We began to think about the problem of snubs after reading a paper by Turner, 'Words, Utterances and Activities'.[3] His conception is worth detailing.

From a stretch of talk Turner extracts the assertion that the talk shows its character as 'complaining'. That is, what is really being done is complaining, and the task of the analyst is to describe the possibility of such a hearing. Here is the piece of talk which occasioned his analysis:[4]

Bert: Yeah, yeah, that's correct. I uh uh really did know hi and uh he was with me in the Alexander Psychiatric Institute in in Alexander, Western Province. I I don't remember his name but we uh we always buddied

[2] For another and, for us, a more interesting view of criticism, see Martin Heidegger, *What Is a Thing*, New York: Henry Regnery Co. 1968, pp. 119–21.

[3] Roy Turner, 'Words, utterances and activities', in Douglas, ed., *Understanding Everyday Life*, Chicago: Aldine, 1970, London: Routledge & Kegan Paul, 1971, pp. 169–87.

[4] Ibid., p. 176.

around together when uh we were at the hospital and we always ((   )) French. And uh I saw him out at Western City about three weeks ago, and I said to 'm, 'Hello, howarya doing?' He said 'I don't know you—who are you?' 'Well, lookit,' I said, 'you *must* know me.' He says, 'No, I don't know you.' Now he was with another fellow there too—waal he didn't want to admit that he was in a mental hospital uh in a hospital—he didn't want to admit it to the other fellow that was with him. So he just walked off and that was it. He wouldn't say hello to me. He wouldn't say nothin'.

Rob: What was your view there? Do you have your own views on that? A touchy point.

Bert: Uh.

?: ((   )).

Jake: Perhaps he didn't like the idea of being in that place. Maybe he didn't want/

Bert: Well no he had to say it—there was another fellow with him you see/

Jake: Well he didn't want to admit/

Bert: Who hadn't been in a mental hospital probably, and he *was* in the hospital. He didn't want *him* to know.

Art: You mean he   )

?: This other guy   )

Couns: But he   )

Bert: Oh, oh never been in a hospital)

Bert: He didn't want to know his friends.

Some might suggest that they hear the talk as 'teaching', 'convincing', 'bringing up to date' or the like. Some might argue that *any* hearing is in principle possible. We submit that we are not compelled to make a decision about the correct hearing rule (as if there was one) for this stretch of talk. If Turner is to demonstrate that this talk is formulable as complaining he has to show us (1) rules for seeing complaining; (2) a grammar in terms of which complaining is usable, applicable, seeable; (3) a community or game within which complaining is conceivable as a move. All of these would also have to be done for any other formulation of the talk, whether as teaching, convincing, or whatever.

The fact is, Turner does not analyse complaining, he analyses snubbing. He glosses off an analysis of complaining in this way: he takes the production of snubbing as one set of grounds for seeing the talk as complaining, while he avoids an analysis of the conditions necessary for hearing a description of a snub as a complaint. Turner's analysis could be read to describe (1) what snubs are; (2) why a particular snub occurred (although these two issues are concretely independent, they are not analytically distinct for us, see below).

We might in this regard criticise Turner for claiming to analyse complaining where he really does an analysis of snub. We shall not do so, however. Instead we will attempt to grasp his analysis of snub.

Turner remarks, almost off-handedly, that a snub or slight takes the form of refusal of recognition. We could read Turner as follows: snub equals a refusal of recognition. Refusal of recognition is an ambiguous notion in several senses. Note in the following how Turner equates snubs and refusal of recognition.[5]

Bert tells his listeners that on recognising the other party he said to him, 'Hello, howarya doing?' Now given that he has already indicated *that* (and *how*) they were acquainted, a greeting is seen to be in order, and to require a greeting in return, since an exchange of greetings is a procedure permitted among acquainted persons; and upon one party offering a greeting, the other is taken to be under obligation to return it. In short, I take it that Bert is invoking what I have just stated in the form of a 'norm', and that it is by reference to such a procedure that it becomes 'obvious' to his listeners that 'something was wrong' when instead of the greeting the greeted party returned with 'I don't know you—who are you?' That this is the case is further provided for by Bert's remark 'He wouldn't say nothin'.' As I understand Bert's remark, assumption of shared knowledge that a greeted acquaintance has an *obligation* to respond with a greeting is both a requirement and a resource for seeing how Bert is entitled to say 'He wouldn't say hello to me', in that he is thus providing for his listeners to find the 'absence of a greeting' to be motivated act.

[5] Ibid., p. 181.

So far, then, we have an account of a breached norm, i.e., the norm that requires acquainted persons to acknowledge one another on meeting face-to-face. This component of the account constitutes the occurrence of a 'trouble', i.e., a 'snub'.

To summarise Turner's argument here: 1. Greetings among acquaintances require returns. 2. (Therefore?) An absent return greeting constitutes a rule-violation, which is equated with trouble and (therefore?) with snub. Turner conceives of his materials as displaying the absence of a returned greeting. But what makes the 'failure to return a greeting' (among acquaintances) more than mere 'behaviour', i.e., what gives an absent return greeting its 'meaning' as a snub? This requires some notion of the grammar of a snub. Turner stipulates a solution by asserting that a snub means 'denial of recognition' but he does not formulate this possibility by describing the grammar of snubs such that we can recognise in failure to return a greeting that we have been snubbed. Further, he does not provide for the character of greetings in such a way as to make a consequent denial of recognition (a snub) intelligible.

Note that in conceiving of snub, we are initially constrained by Turner's formulation in this sense: because (as he sees them) his materials deal with the absence of a returned greeting, we are limited to one possible context in which snubbing is done. One could snub, for example, not just by failing to return a greeting but by ignoring an invitation to a party, or a wedding, or even a beheading. The general class of activities within which snubbing is a possibility are probably activities which demand some sort of reciprocity. That there are a variety of such activities suggests that we could begin (1) by imagining some of these, or (2) by restricting ourselves to Turner's paradigm situation. We shall opt for the latter course (but note the reservation).

Not only is it true that other activities besides absent returned greetings can produce snubs, but it is not necessary that an absent returned greeting be seen as a snub, or even that it be seen as a denial of recognition. To take some quite obvious examples, there are several cases where a snub does not occur even though nothing is said in return: Saying 'Hi' in a hallway at work to someone we had earlier engaged in conversation; saying 'Hi' to a collection of co-workers in the morning, when

113

no one in particular is the responsible (needs to respond) recipient, and so forth. Thus, the possibility of a snub is not in the words 'Hi' or 'Hello' or in a particular body gesture or in the absence of a return greeting because these matters do not always require replies. But there are limits in the other direction too, though perhaps less obvious. Imagine someone returning home from the wars and saying 'Hi' to his lover. Even if you can picture such a thing, would you call that 'Hi' a greeting? If it is a greeting, would a significantly absent response properly be called a snub? (Think of the headline here: 'Mom snubs Oedipus.') The commitments represented in snubbable activities seem not to be very 'shallow' nor very 'deep'. (Thus the joke in conscription notices which begin 'Greetings from the President.')

Turner's analysis can be summarised as follows: a snub is produced as a recognisable affair when a member decides that a greeting which he had directed to another has not been returned, signalling that the other denies recognition. Pulling this apart: a snub consists of (a) a greeting to an acquaintance, (b) which is not returned, (c) when the absence of such a return shows itself as a denial of recognition, and (d) where the denial of recognition can be seen as a snub. In terms of Turner's own account, an ordinary member has to know what it is to decide (a)–(d); he has to know and orient to the conditions under which (a)–(d) become intelligible and relevant. What is glossed in Turner are the grounds in terms of which (a)–(d) become intelligible as possibilities; *that* they are intelligible is not in question, but rather how they are. We will discuss these deep grounds later. Here we want to note that even in the most obvious sense, (a)–(d) can be conceived to be problematic activities for a member. To do (a), an actor must know what it is to give a greeting and must assume that alter knows the same. Among the conditions for an adequate greeting are ego's knowledge that alter is a greetable person (that he is eligible, in position), that alter knows him (that he is possibly recognisable to alter) and that his purpose of 'giving a greeting' is identifiable in the movements and noises he makes. To do (b), ego must know and assume alter to know that greetings require returns or that ego's greeting assigns to alter the responsibility to respond. For (c), ego must assume that the return greeting is absent and he must assume that alter knows it is absent; ego must know how to differentiate between a mere 'missed signal' and a significant absence, i.e., that the absence shows itself as (something like) a motivated denial of recognition rather than something that just happened to occur.[6]

Finally (and Turner ignores this by stipulating that denial of recognition and snub are identical), ego has to know enough to decide that the denial of recognition (which he assumes the absent greeting to mean) shows its character as a snub (d). Our point is that to equate snub with an absent returned greeting, or with denial of recognition, is merely to point to surface features of particular snubs rather than to describe the deep structure which makes possible any decision (including Turner's) that a snub has occurred. That (a)–(d) can be conceived of as problematic activities suggests that Turner's analysis is just a description of some features of a particular snub rather than an analysis of how a snub is possible.

Turner protects the grammar of snub from being explored by showing an interest in particular snubs. His analysis is directed to how snub is used and generated, how it is assembled and accomplished, how it comes to *appear* organised. This type of analysis is necessarily involved in how ideas become organised appearances (i.e., present and graspable) for members, and it is articulated in speech which formulates 'rules' in depicting such organisations. On the other hand, we want to point to the kind of world which supports the idea of snub and to show how this very analysis (this kind of analysis) is a feature of such a world not because it makes 'assumptions' or 'pre-suppositions', but because it treats the idea of snub like a thing, in the same way as those (like Austin) whom it criticises. Discussion between proponents then becomes political rather than dialectic, because attention is focused upon the best way of organising speech to produce simplified versions of ideas.

We have suggested that to see a snub an actor must know how to decide that a failure to return a greeting *is* a denial of recognition and we have already noted that such a decision requires a method for seeing that an absent return greeting is significantly absent. Mere absence does not solve the problem of seeing a snub. It just pushes the problem into another form. It is

[6] Although Turner discusses the issue of motives for this particular concrete snub, he does not treat motive as analytically necessary to the designation of snub in the first place.

115

necessary, therefore, to try to provide for the recognition of a significant absence.

To decide that an absence is significant is to be able to conceive of it (the absent return greeting) as an instance of social action (oriented to an order and governed thereby in its course). Thus to say that a return greeting is absent requires an actor's decision as to whether purpose is assignable to the absence. Since anything can be identified as absent at any given moment, the problem of absence is to see it as significant, i.e., as that which *ought* to be present. To decide this question is to have recourse to a sophisticated notion of what belongs together. The actor must have a method for formulating the absent return greeting as a normatively ordered occurrence, that is, what ought to be present is absent for a reason.

Ego requires some method for deciding that alter was 'free' to return the greeting. Given alter's availability to be greeted (and the possible accompanying conditions), the extenuating circumstances which could prevent alter from freely responding are decided to be absent (alter is not incognito, not joking, etc.). Ego has to assume that alter could have responded (could = had opportunity, capacities, etc.) and this assumption is a parameter of 'denial of recognition'. To say, 'his failure to return my greeting expresses a denial of recognition' is to say that he was free to return my greeting, even though he did not perform such a return. Thus, ego has to decide why, given the absence of obstacles, alter failed to return the greeting. This question raises the possibility for ego of the availability of a rule of relevance for making this absence intelligible. Ego assumes that there exists some set of possible grounds for alter's failure to respond (some possible account), i.e., a possible relevance which could make alter's absent return greeting intelligible if he is assumed to act with reference to the relevance as a rule.

For an absent return greeting to be seen as a denial of recognition, then, it must be seen that alter *chose* not to return the greeting. (But what kind of choice is it? That problem will be addressed below.) That some greetings are not returned seems to be contingent upon two general factors: (1) That conditions of failure for receiving a greeting are present; (2) That a denial of ego's claim for recognition has occurred. (1), while it is an absent greeting, is not a denial of recognition. Alter may not

116

hear the greeting (he is distracted, there is too much noise, etc.) or he may have forgotten that he 'knows' ego (ego no longer wears braces and eyeglasses, ego is mousy and not memorable).

Just as we showed that every failure to return a greeting need not be seen as a denial of recognition, we can show that every denial of recognition need not be seen as a snub. Denial of a recognition does not catch the force of snubs for us, or (as we see them) for ordinary members: the denial of recognition must in some sense be seen as insulting, which requires ego to know, and to presume alter to know, that the denial of recognition is not due to the fact that alter is a spy, or is incognito and wants to temporarily protect his identity, but that the denial is alter's recognisable method for showing that ego is not the kind of person with whom he (alter) wants to affirm a relationship. But we have not yet provided grounds for seeing a denial of recognition (or any other activity for that matter) as alter's method for showing ego that he (ego) is not the kind of person with whom alter wants to affirm a relationship. In other words while we have described, to some extent, how a failure to return a greeting could be seen as a denial of recognition, we have not shown how denial of recognition could be seen as a snub. Or: we still have just a concrete account of snubs.

Take the following:

A: Hi
B: Who are you?

If A is saying something like, 'I know you', then B might be saying something like, 'I do not acknowledge knowing you'. Could B be saying something like: we have not yet been provided with conditions which would permit me to recognise our previous encounter(s) as adequate grounds for recognition (for example not having a proper introduction in our history)? We are suggesting that, if A's 'Hi' is to be potentially snubbable it can not be a request that B remember, a testing of B's capacities to do accurate remembering. Neither can A be asking B to ratify their relationship (in the restricted sense of deciding whether they have one at all). A must *assume* that conditions of history and memory are fulfilled, and thus cannot be construed as asking for a report if he is to be snubbed. This is to say that greetings are neither questions nor requests for information and thus, snubs are neither answers nor self-reports.

Consider something passed up by Turner. When ego gives a snubbable greeting, he imposes upon alter something more than the requirement to respond to a question. Thus, if A's 'Hi' is construed as 'remember me?', B could be seen as having to do a self description (a description of what he remembers). However, this cannot be the force of snub, although it is a denial of recognition. So, 'Hi' as 'remember me' would be a move in a different game than snubbing. We say this because for A to recognise that he has been snubbed by B is first to assume that he is recognisable to B, that B certainly 'knows' him, (of course, he could be wrong, etc., but this is something to be worked out, or to be shown by certain forms of greeting, e.g., 'Hi . . . I am Joe Bunz . . . I used to be your babysitter when your family lived on Roscoe Street'). The point is, that in order for A to produce the recognition of a snub, he has to know that the various conditions which would prevent B from recognising him are absent and that B does in fact recognise him. Thus, when A says 'Hi' he is not saying (asking) 'Do you remember me?' but rather 'I know that you remember me. Show it.' A has to assume that he is memorable to B.

However, note a common occurrence. A says 'Hi' and gets no acknowledgment. A then proceeds to search out possibilities such as that he (A) is not memorable to B, B cannot recall him, he is not distinguishable. We imagine that A does not use 'snub' on such occasions although he might reflect on the possibly worse fate of a non-entity. We want to say that whenever A greets, he assumes recognisability to B. Secondly, A assumes that B knows that A assumes possible recognisability, and thus, A assumes that he is not read as directing a causal or historical query, and that B knows this even if he believes A to be mistaken.

If A's greeting can be construed as 'You know me. Show it.' and B decides to withhold, what do we have? (1) Possible circumstances which might prevent B from responding are assumed to be absent, so that he could respond. (2) B might be construed as lying, for A assumes him to know. But (2) begs the question, for why is he seen as having to lie? If someone knows you in the sense that you assume he knows you and that you assume that he knows you know that he knows you, lying does not adequately capture the activity. It seems that when B says 'No . . . I don't know you' when A assumes he does and assumes that B knows that A assumes that he does, that B is saying something like 'Of course I know you, but I don't want to. I will not treat our (putative) togetherness as authoritative (analytically binding)'.

How did we move from 'No, I don't know you' to 'No I don't want to know you'? Simply this: *given A's assumption that B knows him, B's denial is not taken as a descriptive assertion (about B's mind, what B knows, their history together, etc.) but as expression of reflexive responsibility*, given the fact (A's assumption) that no circumstances prevent B from acknowledging, A is free to take this expression as a statement about their futures together. B's 'I do not know you' is taken as 'You are not the kind of person I want to know'.

Notice now that it is not only that 'denial of recognition' (Turner's version of snub) glosses 'snub' but that snub is not adequately depicted as 'denial of recognition' at all. Rather snub *is* a recognition, a recognition that alter knows ego, wants ego to know that he knows him, yet withholds reciprocity.

Our analysis of snub is not nearly complete. That this is so can help reveal what we take to be an adequate analysis. Staying with Turner, we can ask how we now see *his* analysis of snubs.

As we see him, Turner has not transformed the perspective of a practical member, i.e., he has produced a concrete account of snub in at least these senses: (1) He does not produce methods for seeing an absent return greeting as a denial of recognition. (2) He does not produce methods for seeing a denial of recognition as a snub. In these senses our analysis might be seen as what—an improvement? Deeper than Turner's analysis? Realise in this regard that when we 'accuse' Turner's analysis of being concrete, we are not accusing it of being particular rather than general, but of glossing where it could produce, of refusing to abandon the perspective (the surface perspective) of the practical member. This refusal is seen in the effort to preserve at every step the authority of ordinary usage.

One of the problems here is that Turner attempts to provide an analysis of Bert and probably sees his task as reproducing whatever Bert comes to say. One feature of Bert's talk as Turner sees it is that Bert tries to provide for the practical recognition of snubbing. We, unlike Turner, are not a bit interested in Bert's performance in this context. For us, Bert

119

is an occasion for theorising, just as an International Congress of Sociology might be an occasion for giving a paper. Bert's discussion merely summons up for us some of the possibilities for doing snubbing, but his talk constitutes no principled limitation on how snubs will (finally) appear to us. Turner, sometimes in spite of himself, stays riveted to Bert's talk; our struggle is to get away from Bert's talk. Clearly to say this is to say something different than that our analysis is better or deeper than Turner's. What *are* we saying here?

Turner's analysis (and so far our 'critique') is concrete in a sense other than that it is too superficial. Turner's analysis does not address or even attempt to address its own production. It exempts itself from the very features of talk which it examines through Bert.

The heart of the matter is the idea of membership. Turner is worth quoting on this issue at some length:[7]

A. *The Sociologist inevitably trades on his members' knowledge in* recognizing the activities that participants to interaction are engaged in; e.g., it is by virtue of my status as a competent member that I can recurrently locate in my transcripts instances of 'the same' activity. This is not to claim that members are infallible, or that there is perfect agreement in recognizing any and every instance; it is only to claim that no resolution of problematic cases can be effected by resorting to procedures that are supposedly 'uncontaminated' by members' knowledge. (Arbitrary resolutions, made for the sake of easing the problems of 'coding', are of course no resolution at all for the present enterprise.)

B. The sociologist, having made his first-level decision on the basis of members' knowledge, must then *pose as problematic* how utterances come off as recognizable unit activities. This requires the sociologist to *explicate the resources* he shares with the participants in making sense of utterances in a stretch of talk. At every step of the way, inevitably, the sociologist will continue to employ his socialized competence, while continuing to make explicit *what* these resources are and *how* he employs them. I see no alternative to these procedures, except to pay no explicit attention to one's socialized knowledge, while continuing to use it as an in-

[7] Turner, op. cit., p. 177.

dispensable aid. In short, sociological discoveries are ineluctably discoveries *from within the society.*

As Turner sees his task, his (common-sense) membership needs to be both used and explicated. Explicating means showing how everyone (i.e., all members) comes to see the talk in the same way. *That* members come to see the talk in (more or less) the same way is uninteresting, i.e., a fact. Turner does not feel that he has to show us how *this* is possible, in what game *this* is an intelligible achievement. Also that Turner can *see* his resources (member's resources), that he can state them, argue for them, worry about them, whatever, is not analytically interesting for him but, instead, is merely useful. At some point, Turner treats *his* possibility not as the problem but as a device which allows him to attain a solution. In other words, in spite of what he says, analysis for Turner lies not in explicating the grounds of membership, but in being a member.

Turner's notion (reproduceability) suggests that he wants to impose his notion of snubs (and analysis) on others. He seems to be saying: (1) I 'know' seeings require a method (resources). (2) Therefore let me tell you how I (members) see. But what about a method for understanding how he sees? Isn't it absurd for us to be interested in (even riveted on) his rules if we know (as he tells us) that (1) his rules had to be produced by an unexplicated method; (2) We need a method to see his rules. He assumes that the concrete is available if only he can give rules for seeing it. Imagine in this regard the absurdity of conceiving of Proust trying to impose his image of Albertine on others. The interest of Albertine is as an occasion for showing the nature of seeing (and being). The concrete Albertine, as Proust demonstrates over and over, cannot teach us these lessons. We should treat snubs the way Proust treats Albertine. We should do everything we can to wrench you away from them and towards us, not because we have a 'perspective' but because the notion of perspective is a deceptive palliative. Turner does not transform snubs because, basically, he does not see their *essential* triviality. He maintains a need to see them more carefully (to describe Albertine better than Andrée does) but not to transform them.

In contrast, we do not ask you to reproduce our description; instead we try to show you how to give up that idea. However, we do not do this to substitute the idea that everyone is unique. Instead, in the language we are using here we are recommending that we give up these ideas and move to another level.

It is not that Proust must describe Albertine accurately (or inaccurately) but that he must eliminate her while making every effort to preserve her. We want to show something else, to make reference to something interesting *by* transforming snubs. Turner tries to make snubs interesting but we try to eliminate any lingering interest you might have in snubs (just as Proust does with Albertine). Albertine or snubs are not the point; although they have to be used to make the point.

As we review the analysis so far, it is concrete in that, although it uses grounds (our grounds for constructing the analysis), it does not make reference to them. The remainder of this paper presents (a) rules for seeing snubs, (b) a grammar in terms of which snub is applicable, (c) a community in terms of which snub is conceivable; and presents these only with the intention of making reference to *our* game, i.e., to speak that which makes possible our analysis.

II

An analytic description of snubs is not a description of something that concretely transpires between one person and another but is rather an example of a set of auspices. We may speak of snub and the kinds of acts within which it is a move, but we elect not to treat the move concretely, i.e., not dependent for its cogency on its claim to describe something that has occurred in the world. To a positivist, snub is a contingency in real life; 'understanding' it would mean fleshing out different types of snubs and the situations in which they occur, such that some reader could be persuaded to agree that snubs occur as they are claimed to occur. Instead, we have to display the primordial decision which allows for snub's being seen at all: what authoritative version of analysis allows for the intelligible recognition of a snub as a course of action?

As counterclaim, snubs need first to be made possible by the introduction of an original claim through a greeting. What has not yet been discussed at all carefully is the character of greetings which provide for the possibility of a snub.

What do greetings depend upon for *their* intelligibility? Greetings require before anything else a notion that persons can be different. In this sense, greetings affirm the possibility of distinguishing one person from another. Certain activities, deviance for example, can be done on a desert island, i.e., while deviance may concretely require sanctions, the idea of deviance does not make essential reference to an alter. Guilt, fear, and the like, for example, are appropriate designations apart from the fact that others might apply the terms. It seems impossible, though, to conceive of someone greeting himself in the sense that the greeting could be snubbed. Although they are all common-sense activities (they have this game in common), greetings (and snubs) can be distinguished from deviance in that the former, unlike the latter, *require* a reference to social interaction (to an ego and an alter) for their sense.

It is difficult to provide for a greeting. We only want to locate a greeting that can be snubbed, so we are not concerned with greetings *per se*.

Perhaps we can say that we take the snubbable form of greeting to be an act that requires (to be carried off) that alter acknowledge a public relation to ego. Not 'publicly acknowledge' since a snub can occur whether anyone is around or not, and since clandestine relations are not publicly acknowledged (junkies and pushers, thieves-in-the-night during daytime, lovers, etc.), but rather 'acknowledge a public relation' in the sense that this relation would be intelligible to any man as falling within the realm of possible relations for theoretic members. In other words, a relationship that is acknowledgeable given a community which establishes this.

Assuming that we are right so far, and that a greeting creates the possibility of acknowledging a public relationship, we next need to provide for the character of this relation, since there are some relations that are acknowledged in other ways (paying alimony, serving in the armed forces, etc.) which are not greetings. A greeting is a claim, which to be brought off needs to be acknowledged—it is collaboration plain and simple. But it is a collaboration of a particular sort. A greeting is a claim on alter to collaborate in acknowledging that for present purposes (in the context of this interaction) there are not relevant differences between ego and alter (that potential distinctions between them are specifically irrelevant). In this regard we

I

are suggesting that a greeting is an invitation, however momentary, to suspend differentiation, stratification, evaluation, specialisation.[8] It is to acknowledge only the existence of community in the sense that this community has been created by some (perhaps very minimal) supposed common biography between greeters. It is to claim identity between greeters: however they could be differentiated they shall not be now (through the course of the greeting interaction). This of course is a claim that can be rejected, and this is what happens in snubs. The latter are wilful rejections of the communal claim represented by a greeting.

To review: greetings require the possibility of seeing someone other than oneself. As we have said, one does not greet oneself. So greeting suggests a notion of 'two'. In our analysis so far, the 'two' are of course referred to as ego and alter.[9] But there is also a sense in which greetings require a notion of 'one'. To greet is to say that in some sense we are one. So a greeting requires (1) a notion of difference, (2) a notion of sameness. We might want to formulate this as follows: to greet is to say: although we are different, we share something. But this formulation forces us to ask: if we share something, how are we different?

The problem begins to sound like the old one of social structure and character culture and personality, society and person. We need, for the sense of the analysis, at once to preserve something as different and something as the same. Perhaps: a proper greeting depends upon seeing that someone is concretely different from ego but analytically the same. Greetings require that you see someone as an alter (concretely different) while at the same time you see something as common between you (analytically the same). In this regard, greeters are analytically the same person. This is the meaning of membership. This is how speech line 'Do you remember me?' fails to display a snubbable

[8] Inferiors can use words of greeting to impress or manipulate their superiors, but then they would be doing impression or manipulation and not greeting. This only demonstrates again that it is the grammatic intelligibility and not the terminology which is the essential feature of social intercourse.

[9] In Part I, we treated ego and alter as if they were there to be seen. Now ego and alter are analytic notions which interaction makes necessary.

remark (it is not a greeting), whereas something like 'remember me' is a greeting and so establishes the possibility of a snub.

At the very least this version of greetings clarifies certain conventional sociological issues. Parsons typically raises the social order problem with reference to two actors, i.e., order becomes a problem when there are two actors.

For example:

First a word should be said about the units of social systems. In the most elementary sense the unity is the act. . . . The act then becomes a unity in a social system so far as it is part of a process of interaction between its author and other actors.[10]

or:

The fundamental starting point is the concept of social systems of action. The *inter*action of individual actors, that is, takes place under such conditions that it is possible to treat such a process of interaction as a system in the scientific sense and subject it to the same order of theoretical analysis which has been successfully applied to other systems in other sciences.[11]

or:

(of stable symbolic systems). . . . The most important single implication of this generalization is perhaps the possibility of communication, because the situations of two actors are *never* identical and without the capacity to abstract meaning from the most particular situations communication would be impossible.[12]

What is he saying? That the social order problem can be stated and solved when it is possible to (1) conceive of actors as concretely different and yet (2) analytically the same. Without a notion of analytic sameness there is no solution to the social order problem.[13] Without a notion of concrete difference there is no social order problem at all.[14] Shared norms, and even interaction, become metaphors or cryptic references to the idea of

[10] Talcott Parsons, *The Social System*, New York: Free Press, 1951, p. 24.

[11] Ibid., p. 3.

[12] Ibid., p. 11.

[13] Hobbes, as Parsons reads him.

[14] Cf. works by conventional economists.

analytic sameness. No wonder describing concrete behaviour is so often thought to be sufficient as an example of social interaction.

Greetings with this usage become metaphors or examples of the social order problem. Some social scientists use greetings and similar activities as 'evidence' that social interaction has occurred. They are then saying that to see a greeting is to see the concretely different and analytically identical. In terms of our requirement, for analysis it remains for them to describe how a greeting is possible, since that is what we must see if we are also to understand their claims about social interaction. Parsons, of course, would here invoke, among other things, shared norms. In Parsons, shared norms equal concretely different but analytically the same. In a way, then, invoking shared norms might be Parsons' way of being analytic. But we would direct to shared norms the same question we asked about greetings: how are *they* possible?[15]

III

If greetings are a claim to a kind of sameness then the matter of responding to a greeting means simply that alter collaborate with ego in acknowledging their common identity. It rests on the common-sense assumption that since differentiation is not the issue, anyone could engage in the collaboration since no 'special knowledge' (i.e., differentiated knowledge) is required. One cannot 'beg off', in effect, and give a good reason for doing so. Given that the conditions of failure for receiving a greeting are absent (see Part I), anyone can respond to a greeting. That is precisely the status of a greeting—anyone and everyone can do it if their commitments to one another are not at this point differentiated. That a greeting is not returned, therefore, can only be seen to be a choice not to affirm that they have anything in common (thus 'I don't want to know you').

Returning a greeting therefore depends on the premise that anyone in the community can return a greeting. (Not that any-

[15] It would not be helpful to invoke socialisation here without depicting how a series of temporal events can be collected as an account of shared norms. The same analytic inadequacy is the fate of all descriptively concrete 'explanations'.

one *will*, of course—only that anyone can.) That some greetings are not returned thus is contingent upon two general factors: (1) That conditions of failure for receiving a greeting are present; (2) That the recipient does not acknowledge a public relation. (1) is discounted as having no interest to us if we are interested in snubs. We can say it is not to give a snubbable greeting in the sense that alter is not enabled to provide a response. All in all, then, for a snub to occur it must be seen to be *deliberate*. The original claim for acknowledgment is purposely rejected. (And so another joke in conscription notices which begin 'Greetings from the President'—they cannot be rejected.)

Sometimes that an activity is 'deliberate' suggests that it is also somehow 'difficult'. This is not the case with snubs. Given a greeting has been attempted, a snub is always a possibility. This begins to capture the risk that some people associate with doing a greeting. Just as anyone is in a position to greet, anyone is in a position to snub—anyone can do it. Snubs do not require elaborate training. (Etiquette teaches whom to snub but not how to snub.) No proper exercise of a formal method is required for snubbing. Snubs have a 'simple' character.

If there is anything to the analysis of snubs it is that they must be recognisable and that normal practices permit us to see them. This feature of snubs makes sensible some of our earlier analysis of greetings: understanding the claim of greetings makes possible recognising when that claim is rejected.

Concerning stating snubs and its connection to recognition: think of the acceptability during interaction of saying 'I am snubbing you'. The laughable or redundant quality of the remark is a consequence of the fact that snub is a practice the activity of which itself produces a snub.

We recognise snubs in that we recognise them in their production (an item of which is a greeting) and in no other way. The snub must be 'competent' in this sense; it is perhaps one of the (few?) acts that to be done needs more than an intention. Snubs are not something that are always with us and therefore in order to be reduced are made known by stating them.[16] We

---

[16] As is the case with biases, prejudices, and the like. We are thought to 'own' our biases and so to be intelligible in just the way we intend to be intelligible we are often impelled to state what we possess, a process which permits our hearer to discount what we say in a way that enables him also to know what we say. We do not own snubs.

don't think of snubs as reducible. They are either recognised or not, and if not recognised do not exist.

Unlike lies, snubs are not something to be 'discovered',— they do not exist independently of their noticeability. Lies are conceived to be hidden—it isn't an essential feature of lies that they be noticed. Perhaps a lie is to distort history, snub to reject it. In the original Turner piece Bert may have been snubbed by X in order to lie to his companions (about having been in a mental hospital with Bert).

To be a competent member in common sense requires that we can produce snubs, do so when necessary, and recognise them when done. 'State your snub', as in 'state your bias', is a funny demand, because snubs are conceived to be self-evident in the sense that any member can do them for one thing, and because if they cannot be seen there is no use stating them since they do not exist.

The closest thing to stating a snub comes in apologies; and apologies are very different in that they are requests that what happened should be treated as not having happened. Getting rid of snubs by forestalling them at the source has no status in common sense.

IV

The familiar sociological conception of social action permits us to concretise our discussion.[17]

> Social action, which includes both failure to act and passive acquiescence, may be oriented to the past, present, or future behaviour of others. . . . The 'others' may be individual persons, and may be known to the actor as such, or may constitute an indefinite plurality and may be entirely unknown as individuals. . . . Not every kind of action, even of overt action, is 'social' in the sense of the present discussion. Overt action is non-social if it is oriented solely to the behaviour of inanimate objects. Subjective attitudes constitute social action only so far as they are oriented to the behaviour of others.

[17] Max Weber, *Theory of Social and Economic Organization*, trans. Talcott Parsons, New York: Free Press, 1964, p. 112.

Social action (the recognition of a relationship) require as certain kind of other. This other is not an inanimate thing, nor is it one-self; it is a (non-ego) body other than one-self, while yet being not any body but a body of which certain matters can be assumed. Central to such matters is that the other be a genuine alter which means that he be assumed to have the capacity to take into account one's taking him into account. Thus, ego transforms the idea of otherness into alter when he can assume that other orients to him as an alter. To re-cognise an alter is to formulate him as theoretic, i.e., as re-cognising ego as theoretic. Thus, right off: to identify an alter is to make a claim for theoreticity, for one's being an alter for alter.

To greet an other is to make this claim, for in re-cognising an (theoretic) alter, one presents himself as an alter. In re-cognising the other as alter, one creates himself as an alter for the other. To re-cognise is then to claim theoreticity. The idea of otherness as external to both *ego* and *alter* is obliterated as other becomes what is (now) different from ego.

A greeting makes reference to a claim to theoreticity, a greeting performs a theoretic claim. In terms of Weber's statement, a theoretic claim amounts to this: to say that I am an alter for you is to say that you should take into account my taking you into account. To greet is to make this claim, for it is to say that my taking you into account is worth taking into account.

Snub then becomes intelligible as an icon of the dialectic. It is to deny the claim; it is to be indifferent to the difference between ego and alter when that very difference is presupposed in the encounter; it is to say that his taking one into account is not worth taking into account. In this way, to greet is to propose one-self as an object for a relationship, and to snub is to reject this proposal. But we are still chained by the ordinary conceptions of greeting and snub as reciprocating concrete influences. Let us say that both greeting and snub make intelligible the problem of formulating one-self analytically.

To greet is to propose that one has the analytic status of an alter (which of course presupposes the theoreticity of the One for whom one is an alter). The temptation is then to see snub as a behavioural response to the stimulus of a greeting. Yet snub requires a greeting only in the most trivial sense, for snub really means that the different is not treated as different (his taking one into account is not worth taking into account). In this way, to provide for snubs is to provide for *indifference*. In snubbing, other's claim to theoreticity does not make a difference.

The analytic import of snub, therefore, is not just that it is parasitic upon a greeting. The idea to which snub makes reference is the notion of discriminating. To be indifferent to other is to not invest him with value as an alter, it is to let-him-lie as a thing.[18] Snub becomes a metaphor for de-personalisation, it is a way of drawing a line (of discriminating) between that which makes a difference and that which makes no difference. Whereas the greeting performs a claim about the theoreticity of Self (which presupposes the theoreticity of an alter, or difference), the snub performs a claim about theoreticity of other (which presupposes the theoreticity of Ego). To snub is then not simply to reject a greeting but is to be indifferent to the difference the existence of which must be accredited in order to deny it. Snub says: though I need difference as a resource, I will act as if I do not. Snub is to disregard resources as topics.

Greeting then collects, or does, similarity if by that we mean: our unity resides in your capacity to differentiate me. Similarly, one couldn't greet unless he could differentiate Self as Other. Greeting assumes differentiation and proposes that this be grounds of similarity of sameness. In a comparable way, snub does differentiation if it is understood as a differentiation based upon sameness: this is the claim that our difference presupposes a community equipped with the resources to re-cognise one another. Snub hurts precisely because it is grounded in this sameness—the sameness that permits snubs to be intelligibly recognised. In effect snub says, though you are an alter, you are not worth treating as an alter, i.e., though we share the recognition that you are an alter, this recognition is not worth acting upon.

Snub then appears as a pure case of the diabolical; it is not done out of ignorance but with the understanding that it denies 'what is'. Snub is a pure case of injustice.

To pick up the thread that snubs deny the claim of a greeting, we now want to consider how that denial can be understood as an insult. We have already suggested that snubs (and greetings) require a notion of visible (concrete) 'other'. But the world of

---

[18] A paradigm for the snub can be seen in typical social science research where 'conditions' and 'extraneous factors' are treated with indifference *vis-à-vis* 'variables' (alters).

snubs invests more power in 'other' than just thereness. Notice first of all that snubs are often seen as a trouble—they can 'hurt'. The indignation which accompanies the seeing of a snub is made possible by a form of life which seeks affirmation with or from an other. Within this world snubs are a denial, but they are denials which are made possible only through the power of potential affirmation. (The point here about affirmation of course, is parallel to the one made earlier about greetings.)

The problem of snubs then, is equivalent to the problem of affirming difference or sameness. If sameness, no snub; if difference, snub. But notice that in snubbing, i.e., in differentiation, one is acceding to the existence of something, namely a differentiated alter.

Snubs thus work from the understanding that the character of the victim has been affirmed through a denial. This is to say that snub as a denial of a claim to similarity presupposes an alter to deny and consequently, that in its denial snub at least affirms the existence of alter while rejecting his claim.

Paradoxically the denial becomes a kind of affirmation. And it is not just that to be denied one must be concretely 'there'. It is more that the acceptance of the denial by other as a report about his character is in itself an affirmation that he has a character. In a queer way, one who is hurt by a snub does not see snub for what it is, in that accepting the snub as a report on his character he denies what his very recognition of the snub presupposes.

The assurance one gets from being snubbed seems incongruous: being treated as a non-entity serves to preserve the originally held conception of Self. The queerness of the idea of snub flows from the maintenance of the idea that a contradiction of Self is (1) visible and (2) synonymous with Self. This Self maintains at the same time its nature and the contradiction of this nature as depictions of Self. This is how difference becomes similarity in the language through which snub is intelligible.

The essentially protective nature of snubbing and snub worries is not usually noted. In the positivist world of common sense snub is conceived to be a threat to the victim's character. We are saying, on the contrary, that snubs can be seen as prophylactic, that snubs presuppose an alter toward whom Ego is indifferent. To greet is to offer one-self up to another, to offer to be other than one is. To snub is to reject this offer, to deny that alter is anything but himself. Thus it is Ego who refuses that aspect of dialectic (negativity) which, together with what Hegel and Kojeve call Identity, permits one to be simultaneously what he is for other and what he is for himself.[19] The snubber denies alter this freedom, which is to say he enslaves alter. The worries which obscure this relation keep the dialectic of snubbing a mystery to the concrete theorist.

We proposed earlier that to snub is to say: 'I do not want to know you.' This is probably true, but we can now reformulate 'I don't want to know you' in a way that accords more directly with what we seem to have been doing all along, namely to tie it to the idea of form of life, membership, making reference, solidarity, and the like—to tie the idea of snubs to an interactive collaboration. 'I don't want to know you' is: 'We have nothing in common.' Snub says: the resourceful use of difference constitutes no grounds for topicalising difference and thus, what is used (as ground) has value only as a 'thing' to be left behind.

That a snub says we share nothing does not mean you are nothing. Indeed it affirms that you are something, in this case something with whom the snubber can claim to have nothing in common. Sharing nothing is an assertion of difference, not an assertion of nothing. It is not to be nothing to be snubbed, it is to be different. In this regard both snubber and snubbee recognise that the latter is only and exclusively an other, i.e., in snubs it is selves (of ego and alter) that are conceived by the snubber to share nothing. Although it may be tempting to see snubbers as saying you are nothing, nevertheless they are, by refusing to treat other as anything *but* an other, thereby preserving him as something. In this sense, to 'cut someone dead' is not to obliterate him, as the idiom implies. Although snubs may hurt, they do not kill. Not only do they not kill, they make other perspicuous. They make him perspicuous by calling attention to his exclusive otherness through the claim we have nothing in common. This is the world of definites needed to do snubbing, and in which snubs can be recognised for what they are.

[19] See G. W. F. Hegel, *The Phenomenology of Mind*, trans. J. B. Baillie, New York: Macmillan, 1931; A. Kojeve, *Introduction to the Reading of Hegel*, ed. Allan Bloom, trans. James H. Nichols, New York and London: Basic Books, 1969, pp. 198–201.

To snub is to say we have nothing in common. Recall that greetings were seen to be an affirmation that concrete differences (1) are there, but (2) do not matter. What are snubs? An affirmation of (1), of difference, a claim that I am not the same as you, a rejection of your claim that we are the same.

We might be torn at this point between two different formulations. We could say: if snub is an affirmation of difference, it cannot be an affirmation of concrete difference, because greetings are that. Taking the obvious path here, one would conceive snub as an affirmation of analytic differences. Snub could (1) distinguish concrete from analytic differences, (2) affirm the latter. Snubs become analytic greetings. This captures (what?) the discrimination of the snubber if by that is meant he knows how to organise the materials of interactions so as to keep Other as other.

Another formulation seems better. We have already seen that snub requires an affirmation of difference, a rejection of a claim to sameness. Now we must ask how this sort of affirmation is possible, i.e. what makes this usage analytically adequate. Snubbers accomplish this by analytically collecting concrete differences, thus acting to segregate the snubbed from the snubber. A greeting and its partner, the snub, are actions that issue in and from the problem of solidarity, because they organise the interaction with reference to possible collecting and segregating. In this organisational sense any greeting, any snub, any return greeting is the product of a division of labour which orients and re-enforces its own features: interactional similarity, difference, nothingness, somethingness, self, other, collecting, segregating. It is a member of that family of interests which includes such matters as social class, social deviance, and the like because it requires attention to the dialectic creation and re-creation of the many from the one and the one from the many. In so far as snubs can be seen to be connected to problems of solidarity and integration, so can we say that snubbing is another expression of the one and the many, which is to say it is an expression of the social idea of a division of labour. Snubbing is to organise interaction so as to differentiate persons via the work they do in terms of the interactional division of labour. That is, we can say that the notion 'We have nothing in common' preserves other as something, specifically as an enslaved participant in snubbing interaction oriented to and created by its own foundation in collecting and segregating. The snubber refuses alter's offer to transform the many into a one, leaving alter merely to exist.

This idea has a certain resonance. There is a common-sense idea that there is something improper, even unnecessarily improper, about snubbing someone and we have suggested that it is a calculated, deliberate sort of impropriety. Now the deliberateness can be formulated as a decision to segregate, rather than to collect (a decision to collect difference). It is thought, in snubbing, that the snubber deliberately elects to segregate, since the greeting made it possible for him to do something else, to collect.

We have remarked that we are not interested in doing mere criticism. By this we make reference to the imperfect nature of speech. Concrete speech is not a natural order because it depends for its sense on a collection of unspeakable analytic grounds for that speech to achieve intelligibility. Speech does not objectify its objects—being imperfect, speech cannot be representational. Rather, it is grounded in unspeakable auspices. Writing is to make speech, and if we are to make speech which is not nihilistic chatter we must in our speech make reference to the possibility of Alter. We must collaborate with the reader or hearer by exemplifying the possibility of deep grounds for our speech, such that he can be himself for himself, but also himself for us. We thereby *join* the reader, and negate the mere concrete 'fact' of individuality which in itself would generate a world populated by egos, a world of masters lacking even a slave.

Reading, then, is an enterprise which is the equal of writing in that it is an equally elevated act of grounding what is read which thus enables the writing to go beyond chatter. This awesome responsibility—it is a charge to be analytic—is akin to making one from two by joining the writer and reader in a reflexive collaboration. So it is not an assessment of correctness that we ask of ourselves or our readers, but rather the provision of grounds or auspices, which transforms us all from mutually substitutable two's or ego's into a differentiated collection of ego and alter. We take it that criticism, in so far as it concerns itself with correctness through an unreflexive conception of perfect and self-objectifying speech (writing), is incapable of such a realisation. Kojeve, for example, describes vulgar science as 'carried out by a Subject who pretends to be independent of the object':[20]

> The naive man, the vulgar scientist, even the pre-Hegelian philosopher—each in his way opposes himself to the Real and deforms it by opposing his own means of action and methods of thought to it.

Given imperfect speech, then, reading is a task that requires providing grounds for speech. At this point in the argument it is perhaps redundant to suggest that providing someone's grounds is akin to seeing him as the same as us. We can show how anyone is (deeply) like us. We can show anyone's analytic. Now we can say: this is to say we cannot snub anyone if we are to do our analytic work. Snub means affirming a difference, the way criticism does in opposing the work of an author and its evaluation by reader or critic. It is our view, on the other hand, that analysis as opposed to criticism requires collecting—or differentiating only in order to collect—and consequently the sheer affirming of difference alone is not to do analysis. It boggles our minds to do both criticism *and* analysis, just as it would boggle the mind to do both snubbing and returning a greeting.[21]

Another point: we have a notion that we can analyse anything. This is to say, anything can be seen and shown to fall under our auspices. We really say everyone can be collected as a member of our community although concretely everyone is different from us. Our auspices are the one set that can provide for everyone.

We are beginning to formulate a method for seeing snubbing (and criticism) as unnecessary activities. This matter cannot be addressed in detail here. But notice a kind of unpleasant

---

[20] Kojeve, op. cit., p. 176.

[21] Consider, for example, the 'difference' between more traditional sociologists who state that bias should be eliminated and newer sociologists who affirm bias cannot be eliminated, or even should be eliminated. We could imagine these groups snubbing one another, i.e., affirming their differences. But we have shown that when they affirm their differences they are being concrete. Analytically, they all are the same. We show by collecting them why they (shouldn't) snub each other because they each generate their idea of bias in the same way.

symmetry in the two issues of how a snub could possibly hurt and how a snub could legitimately be done. The same world (here: the concrete world) in which a snub can cause pain (although not too much pain because basically snubs protect) is the one in which snubbing, i.e., being concrete, is a possibly proper action. The same form of life that is bothered by snubs allows them to occur. Suffice it to say that it is possible to conceive of other worlds.

We have used the example of snub to make reference to the dialectic of togetherness and apartness, of re-cognition and discrimination, of integration and differentiation. We have not sought to propose one particular formulation of snub, but to make transparent to resonances which any one formulation masks. We have sought to show that our very method of collecting resonances is supported by a moral order against which the conventional analysis of snub offends and we have pointed to the form of life which underlies snub analysis as itself an extension of the ordinary-un-thinking-life that produces the idea of snub—whether as rebuff, insult, or rejection.

The idea of snub resonates with ideas of restraint, discretion, and limit; to accept the seriousness of snubs is to preserve the limits of a concrete understanding of self (as commodity) as a real limit. It is not that snub is this or that, but that the idea that snub *is* something makes reference to a life in which ideas are converted into things. We have shown another world—a world in which snub is not a thing, is no-thing—by re-organising our conversation around the resonances which resist being transformed into things.

6 TRAVEL

I

At this point, people remain an unexamined issue. We treat evaluation independently of actual authors and referees, snubs as a community independently of people who do and do not snub, and bias as a feature of the scientific community rather than of biased men. But the idea of people, as those bodies who perform and look and refuse recognition and distort science has been neglected.

We shall now take up this idea of people—more precisely, we shall take up activities that can only be understood as ones which are nothing but what they are—through an inspection of travel. We shall explicate travel, but in so doing we use travel as an occasion for showing certain troubles with thinking of the social as people who *do* this and that. We shall show how 'people' concretises life, in that people strictly conceived are groundless events and thus epiphenomena, mere existentials. We are interested in what a report of mere existence would look like, and one way to do this is to examine travel, because the impulse to travel is the impulse to mere existence. Travel, then, is a way of getting at the form of life which would produce a peopled world as the paradigm of a social world. We shall therefore be thinking about participation, movement, the field, observers, visibles, being by oneself, being alone, solitude, loneliness, selflessness, photographs, ego-centricism, change, community. We shall come to understand that existence, as in 'people exist', is the equivalent of groundlessness, of movement without change, a field without ground, a visible without a source, a place without context.

II

We began to think about travel as a result of living in a foreign place, of being strangers in the everyday sense of the term: where one's position is determined essentially by the fact that one does not belong; a position which denaturalises the interactions of the stranger.[1] The pain that attends such living as a routine and sustained problematic made us wonder who would happily choose that mode, and we realised that the traveller does, with the very important exception that the traveller is not required to come to terms with his foreignness, i.e., he does not have to be responsible. The traveller chooses not to belong, and he does not have to care, or be responsible, with regard to the denaturalisation of (his) common culture. This scheme of things, notably a vacation from commitment and constraint, is peculiar; peculiar not in that it is rare, but because it provides an apparent contrast to the kinds of everyday activities we think of as work, home, friendship, teaching, learning and so on. For any place, one can imagine those who wouldn't want to travel there, those for whom it is home. As a holiday, now a holiday from the responsibilities of belonging and therefore a holiday from *some* where, travel is to be anywhere, and to noticeably be anywhere. Travel is to make anywhere noticeable, to notice that one is in a community while not being responsible to it.

That travel is to be anywhere, rather than somewhere, explains some familiar features of the phenomenon. We might

[1] It is perhaps obvious that one does not have to travel to become a stranger, nor does one become a stranger simply by travelling (the businessman). Also, we will soon note that the stranger and the traveller are anything but identical.

138

wonder why good travellers leave places which appear beautiful, interesting and exotic to them, why they leave places which satisfy their avowed desires. The reason is that the traveller's interests in beauty and exoticism are surface versions of his commitment to being anywhere, and so even the beautiful will not attract him for long since he is interested in beauty not as his version of somewhere (community) but as his version of anywhere. Beauty is oriented to by the traveller only in so far as it satisfies his craving for looking. He is not after a beautiful community but after instances of beauty as one way of refusing the commitment to community. In other words he is interested in beautiful things rather than the idea of beauty and his interest in beautiful things exhausts his attention.

Also intelligible are the endless possibilities, the open-ended quality of where the traveller could conceivably go. If it is easy to rule out places as sites for 'homes' but not as sites for travel, it is due to the difference between being at home and travelling. Being at home is to formulate a connection between self and place such that for every (distinctive) self there will be a limited number of potential homes. The case of the man who can be at home anywhere now appears as the man without a self. Since travellers seek not connection but separation, distance and not belonging, anywhere can potentially do. Real travellers feel this anywhere quality of their existence in the frustration of practical limits and their ability to go away. Real travellers with their commitment to anywhere, or anything, are insatiable.

Some people on holiday go from Hilton to Hilton, bearing our disrespect for never visiting the native quarter. They could be anywhere, all right, but they seem to miss the idea that to travel we must make anywhere noticeable, there must be something to see (to notice). Travel has to be peopled. Hence the native quarter. This is how photographs can re-present a trip. Since to travel is to make anywhere noticeable, the essence of a trip is what is noticed, which in turn is what can be photographed. To make anywhere noticeable is to make that which can be seen independent of any ground (not to belong it to anything) and thus what is seen as anywhere, as groundless. To read Baedeker is to make the scene noticeable, by contrast with going from Hilton to Hilton, while at the same time it is only to notice. In travel we establish the possibility of looking and ignore the possibility of a relationship as the responsible re-creation of

139

what we see. Imagine in this context the irresponsible or tourist character of a student who thinks he can adequately re-create a lecture with some photographs. In lecturing the idea is understanding rather than looking, and so photographs cannot re-present the event (if it is an event). Travel is mindless in so far as it exempts its participants from analytic work—it is to be exclusively passive, empty, and without resource. Thus the double meaning of the exhaustion of travel as a state of being barely awake.[2] It avoids the pathos of indigenous cultural poverty and deprivation by having been chosen. The traveller chooses to be deprived—he rejects rather than accepts, and in this respect he is the field-tripper, the sampler, the tourist of the interdisciplinary. He 'shares' his emptiness with the natives, but he is not indigenous in that he cannot, like the stranger, embark on any analytic programme to make anywhere somewhere by authorising some relation between self and place such that he makes reference to a source, to a relation which serves to ground anywhere. The stranger does not just see, but (attempts to) makes a difference by treating what is seen as whatever it *is*, as something with authority. Thus 'I am in London' could be saying 'I am in London' or 'I am in London though I could be anywhere.' It could be saying 'I am a Londoner' or 'I am travelling in London.' The former is an inhabitant, he seeks in the looking. The latter is a tourist, he looks without seeking. The new as a concern of both stranger and traveller represents change and movement, respectively. Perhaps this is why travellers often seem brave to natives. The traveller is willing to try anything, to have 'adventures' precisely because he has no stake at all in what may happen to him. Really he is not brave so much as indifferent. Having no self and being anywhere, what happens is all the same to him. Travel cannot broaden, except in the way a laundry list can be a long one, because nothing can be sought in travel and hence nothing happens to the traveller.[3] It is becoming clear now how the traveller may explicate the idea of the person: the traveller

---

[2] Again, we are not disapproving of travel, simply trying to inspect what it is. Each of us travels and likes it in certain concrete ways.

[3] It is probably unnecessary at this point to remind the reader that a traveller can become a stranger, and vice versa, and so one who sets out to travel can learn something because he has turned himself into a stranger.

is strictly personal, can only take it personally, can only see the personal, since he ignores the source of embodied activities. He sees only what his eyes look at. Furthermore, as a fundamentally irresponsible, uncommitted type, the traveller (like the participant observer) wants to see without being seen (sometimes to be seen without being responded to, which is another version of the same). So being seen, even as a tourist, is to make possible some kind of discussion of who is who and what is what: to consider what one is doing, to acknowledge that what one's eyes see is partly produced by who one is. Travellers find that kind of realisation unpleasant because it implies just the sort of commitment to explication, understanding, and grounding which they are trying to avoid.

Think of travel writing as distinct from inhabitant writing. The best travel writing is a description of place such that it is accessible to anyone (anywhere), i.e., it is writing formulated so as to require no analytic and therefore differentiated understanding. Which is to say that the best travel writing is probably the worst writing: hotels, food, itinerary, sights—nouns, usually proper nouns, the visibles, the way people are visibles. They are visibles because it is the thingness of the thing that can be seen, the way a baby needs a name, which is what is recommended to our attention (we are awake so we can attend). Travel writing is a description meant to stand independently of language, hence its thingness as rules of thumb which qualify as anyman's guide.

The places and the names of those places stand to one another as a relation of independent and dependent variables. It thus becomes only a technical matter of finding the right word or name for depicting the place to be named, e.g., 'the beaches at Mombasa are warm during the winter and hot during the summer', 'the ramparted village of San Gimignano is fourteenth-century and a romantic paradise', and so on. No such thing as a writer's commitment accompanies the itinerary. The writer often evaluates of course, which is implicit in the above remarks and explicit when he says 'the beaches at Mombasa are whiter and sandier than the beaches at Dakar.' But this is not to examine the idea of excitement[4] that is travelling and looking, it is

---

[4] Excitement is synonymous with the exhaustion discussed earlier. Travelling is exciting to the degree it is exhausting. This exhaustion often comes to be called boredom, and can be perceived among exhausted–bored museum lookers.

to accede to it; it is for the writer to become a traveller. It is to accede to a distinction while choosing to ignore making the difference that would ground the distinction. To compare travel writing with naming the baby is thus only a slight joke. One's preference is indeed a preference, but one does not maintain his grasp of the writing as travel writing if he seeks the commitment which introduces the preference, which makes the preference accessible. Here again we run up against the groundlessness of travel. And isn't it fair to say that this would also be a description of a merely peopled world, a world of preferences for states?[5] A travel writer can have a 'point of view', as can the traveller. To be analytic then, as in being a stranger as distinct from a traveller, is not equivalent to having a point of view. Point of view, in other words, does not obviate groundlessness. Cathexis is nothing if not to distinguish, while failing to authorise the distinction; a traveller's focus on cathexis is the treatment of any distinction as a matter of usage, a matter of what is and is not cathected. The problem here, such as it is, would be to isolate and describe the various things so cathected, and to isolate and describe the various things so cathecting. 'Americans are anal-aggressive' is in this sense analytically identical to 'the beaches at Mombasa are white and sandy.'[6] So another turn comes to be the tourist, now a professional, who makes a life out of travelling among his own without quite knowing, or seeming to know, what he is doing.

There is a reason for the hyperbole of travel advertising besides the self-aggrandisement of the industry. Superlatives are exactly what the traveller wants, since that is what is most exciting in a world where difference is everything. Moderation is boring to the traveller.

Seeing slides of someone's travels—better, seeing slides as anyone's slides—is always a bore and a joke. This is because they are only the pictures of the owner of the pictures. They are only the words of the actual speaker, they incorporate no claim to make reference to how the words could be language. They

[5] Note we permit a peopled world to be composed of oriented people, so our argument is not reducible to the one, beginning with Weber, which requires that actors be oriented before we have a sociological phenomenon. A traveller can be oriented, so an oriented actor is not the idea we have in mind here as a contrast to a peopled world.

[6] Identical if 'Americans are anal-aggressive' is taken to be a description by looking which requires no authorising commitment.

denote the common—buildings, a sunset—rather than what brings us together: the communal intention needed to see that sunset as an icon of authority which grounds our relation in that sunset. There is nothing 'wrong' with slides, of course. Actually they are perfect markers for travel, they do not contradict the entirely personal character of travel, which is why they are always dull. Travel pictures are only speech, only buildings and people, not language. They are the visibles, indigenous to no language. In this regard travel is clearly ego-centric, neither 'me' as the alter of a relation nor 'I' as the maker of a relation. The traveller gets along fine with his phrase book, the stranger finds it laughable.

The traveller's commitment to speech rather than to language explains why he doesn't mind and may even prefer being in places where he doesn't understand the language. Noise or sound is better than language in the same way that the eye is better than the mind.

III

In travel then, I can only be conceived as a man, a singularity, exclusively a one. Where the stranger may not be a member in the existential sense, this is the very issue which creates the stranger, namely the *possibility* that he is only a one, and there-fore the possibility that he may be a One. The traveller, on the other hand, is only and exclusively a person, a *thing* in the way that buildings, sunsets, words are things. That he can be a One is not a contingency. To be in a community is to be somewhere: to dissolve the personal in the identity and resource of a unity rather than the singular existential. To travel is to be anywhere: to look, to be indifferent, to be sourceless. 'I want to go some-where warm' is to say 'I want to go anywhere warm', to declare a preference, and when one goes it doesn't change the world, it doesn't touch the world really, it is not to move in the way going home, going to work, or emigrating is movement. It is not a movement toward, or movement away. Travel is a commit-ment to the maintenance of the entirely new; once we perform an analytic on a place we absorb it into (an analytic) tradition and thus it can no longer be just a fresh object. The thing—home, workplace, nation—is changed by displaying its source.

These are the very matters that many recognise as the matters to be escaped through the option of travel as sheer movement. Some persons, for example, are thought to travel because they are troubled and need to get away. But to get away from what? From their pain, apparently. Given that travel can be escape (by being singular rather than communal), will travel change anything, even if the pain disappears? That is, do we look for surcease or understanding, for an escape from pain or for that which authorises our ability to seek pain? The movement from fear which is escape can only make something (which could have been suffering the pain) into nothing (travel, anywhere). So travel is different, escape from pain is different, in that it takes that which makes a difference (something) and turns it into that which can make no difference (nothing). Escape from pain is nihilistic because it obviates any understanding of the pain itself, i.e., it prevents us from transforming the pain into suffering. Travel, as escape from pain, is the equivalent of oblivion. The traveller seeks oblivion. The analyst who would turn the world into one peopled by travellers seeks to obliterate. Being an obliteration, the turning of something into nothing, it can hardly be revolutionary because it does not transform. In fact it is the antithesis of revolution. It is to treat death as the only option with full knowledge that there is an available life solution, which is to say that it is a perfectly cynical choice.[7] It is to choose death.

To run from pain is to be possessed. To gain surcease from pain, or trivialities like weather, is to be possessed in that the person is governed by the state he possesses: pain, warmth, cold, and the like. We 'own' our states, since they can only be our own states in any strictly ego-centric world. What we are is whatever our states are, there being no community that could authorise a relationship by which we could seek to understand our being-states. We are thus possessed, being no more than the states we have. Possessed in a purely ego-centric world, we arrive yet again at another display of the crisis of capitalism and

[7] Perhaps we need a reminder here that we start with the idea that being physically dead or physically alive has no self-evident analytic status, so neither does going from one physical state to the other—we have to provide the sense, whatever it may be. Sheer movement for us is the failure to recognise this, the failure to *make* the difference that would be analytic change instead of physical movement, the failure to authorise any difference.

144

its focus upon the thing (the pain), a focus which obliterates the human possibility (to understand the pain, and thus to suffer). The impulse to travel is the impulse to treat pain as mere pain and so to seek relief rather than understanding. It is to seek mere exchange, one state for another, warmth instead of cold.

Travel as cathexis—the personal—may explain the very difficult problems that come up when one travels with others. Since travel is declaring preference it always conflicts with sharing, communicating, relating. Travel exists in a world of charms so it is always difficult for one to travel with others, since as others they have preferences too. Arguments and splits are not accidental features of travel but part of the basic idea that the two travelling are two one's rather than one two. Solutions that travellers regularly produce, e.g., compromise, spending the afternoon alone, are solutions which reveal the basic problem. The personal, cathecting character of travel is also revealed in the very limited kind of talk travellers *qua* travellers can produce. Since travelling is declaring preference, travel talk is merely preference talk, self-expression, exclamations and disclamations. In another sense, then, we can see travel as being anti-dialectic. As usage and cathexis, talk by travellers and travel-writing are singularly inarticulate. They are expressive, exclamatory rather than saying. Similarly, the fact that the traveller's distinctions are not authorised provides another version of why good travellers can go anywhere. The world is not divided in any absolute sense into good and bad since for the traveller good and bad are equivalent to mood, whim, and momentary sense impression. Hence it is often hard to repeat the experience because it is momentary.

The potential marriage of state and preference is the interest of the traveller and thus could be said to express the ubiquitous idea of 'the actor's point of view'. However, the traveller will not understand even this because it requires him to see his trip as grounded in self, which he does not want to recognise. The fact that travel cannot be repeated might lead someone (but not a traveller) to realise that travel is dependent on self. The traveller thinks he can repeat his trip because he conceives of himself not as self but as mindless eyeballs. This is not to say, of course, that concrete travel will not give occasion to reflect, to avoid oblivion. The point is rather that even when these occasions occur, the traveller does not try to formulate. Thus

145

there is the traveller's regret that places lose their character and surely this is a result of travel but the traveller does not want to use incidents like these to reflect on the nature of travel but rather as matters for regret.

In that the traveller seeks relief rather than understanding, he can treat any 'problems' that occur during his trip as the problems of place or state rather than of self. For travellers then, real problems are occasions like bad weather, bad food, and unfinished hotels. If self is brought into the matter at all it is only as the receptacle which relieves the state. So, for the traveller, problems of self are things like dysentery and tired feet, which, as he sees them, stop him from gaining the relief or escape he is seeking. Because it is a world of relief but not understanding, what cannot occur in a traveller's world is reflection about the real source of the problems: not rainy weather or dysentery, but the form of life which makes everything depend upon such triviality.

IV

Travel continually clarifies the disconnections between change and movement. If you live in New York and travel to Morocco does that mean there is nothing to see in New York? And who would not travel to Morocco? Moroccans would not travel to Morocco, nor New Yorkers to New York. For anyplace, there are those for whom it is home, those for whom the movement of travel would not be possible. One sees something different (Morocco rather than New York) not because the place has changed but because one has changed places. Movement does not change the world, one might say it does not touch the world, and if it does not touch the world how can it touch the self?[8] Community, coming together, resources of interaction, and the like are not necessary to our thinking about the drift that is travel. The individual can be thought to travel independently of his relations, as it were.

Travel truly brings men back in, turns them into people in so far as we recognise the activity without also recognising how

[8] Actual travel may change real selves, but this would not then be analytic travel. Voyages of discovery are quite possible, and often occur at home, e.g., for Moroccans in Morocco.

that activity comes to display something other than itself. Travel stands to the social as speech to language. Its groundlessness is the equivalent of talk without a referent. The very thing of interest about being a tourist is that one knows he is in a community of language but not of it, being only a looker. Thus, for example, the appellation 'tourist' for those who only visited student controlled buildings during university confrontations. To travel is not to be a brute, for the brute does not know what he does. Travel is a refusal, a refusal to join, and in this analytic regard a New Yorker can become a tourist in New York, etc. That is, we can think of a world populated exclusively by tourists and such a world is a purely peopled society: barely awake, irresponsible, uncommitted, babbling. In a word, nihilistic. It is a world that is generated, moreover, by sheer bad faith, for it is chosen in the knowledge of other possibilities. We cannot offer the same excuse for it that we do for brutes, strangers, children, and psychotics.

Given that one can remain a tourist at home, or become a member abroad, we can see that activities like field trips, ethnography, interdisciplinary studies, dating, going out, and so forth never acquire community at face value. In fact, the idea of face value, in so far as it is the rhetoric of travel, can never make reference to the social. Neither can the limited idea of point of view. To see a person, for example, is only to see more furniture, something which may offer various Hobbesian uses but no relations. The field trip to prison is an aesthetic solution to (what?) the possibility of difference: look and it will show itself. Is this participant observation, ethnography, where participation is conceived to be a goad to the population to show itself? If so, it shares a great deal more with demography than has been realised, namely that the observer–demographer makes it impossible to join, to become we. Our observer–demographer–field-tripper has become a capitalist. By contrast:[9]

Man is truly human (that is, free and historical) only to the extent that he is *recognised* as such by others and that he himself recognises them in turn. . . . Hence Man can be truly human only by living in society.

[9] Alexander Kojeve, *Introduction to the Reading of Hegel*, ed. Allan Bloom, trans. James H. Nichols, New York: Basic Books, 1969, pp. 235–6.

147

The participant observer enters into some sort of contact with his subjects, the student with his interdiscipline, and so on. They talk, they theorise, they write. But the traveller does, too. Again, it is what one takes this contact to be: a dialectic of mutual recognition within a community of language, or a monologue by some speaker. Counting the number of interactions between natives, for example, any tourist could accomplish, no matter how technically sophisticated he may have to be by way of differentiating eye-glances, discovering surreptitious meetings, etc. What authorises the count, in that it joins the observer and native by reference to the possible membership remains the issue.[10] This is the difficulty with 'non-reactive measures'—are they not to recognise, and be recognised? If one does not obtrude, one fails to change; he makes no difference, he is nothing. Hence the chattel crisis, the subordination of men to things, the loss of any means to express our freedom from the states in which we find ourselves.

What we can like about field reports and travel writing is that they supply us with an infinite collection of possibilities—better, *we* must supply them with the possibility of an infinite collection of possibilities. Travel writing and field notes do not stand under any ground, we are not expected to seek any such constraint in the writing. We are 'free' in the worst sense, free to own the writing, to control it absolutely, there is no other with which to come to terms. We avoid the pain that accompanies the search for commitment which is understanding.

V

Travel has often been an object of theorising. That is, the being of travel—what it is—has been the object of countless explications. In this way, travel has been formulated as Real change. What we have proposed is that the change is more apparent than Real, that it is actually movement and not change at all.

[10] Their common membership does not have to be concrete, say as the village or family are. We have already discussed this with regard to naming, such as happens in families. Common membership could be 'simply' an exchange of traditions, or ideologies—whatever would ground the contact that is only speech in the resources of language which generate that speech.

Travel then has served as an opportunity to address the ideas of change and motion and the question of what kind of world allows motion and movement to be taken as change.

Theories of travel as re-presented in the writings of men like Bacon, Montaigne, Hume, and others all recommend the educational effects of travel, i.e., that travelling ought create Real change (the change which we might speak of as learning). This assumed connection between movement (changing places) and learning is mediated by theories which stipulate that movement reorganises the soul by exposing it to what is different. Yet the difference revealed by a new place (by change of places) can only be a difference connected to place and hence, not a difference at all. Differences connected to place are observed features of places which acquire relevance when noticed. Consequently this idea of difference equates change with noticing.

In the idea of travel which we are examining, place loses its analytic weight and becomes a position or point from which to view. Thus, when Heidegger says, 'the old meaning of the word "end" means the same as place' and that 'from one end to the other means: from one place to the other' because end points to the place 'in which the whole is gathered in its most extreme possibility,'[11] he is showing the analytic sense of place as the completion or gathering of the limit of an idea. To change is to gather together the essence of the idea at its limit, i.e., to bring the idea to its fulfilment. Real change is to engage in that gathering—to occupy that place—which is no particular place but anyplace. In contrast, the idea of change which we have been examining sees change as movement from place to place.

The idea of travel as a source of change converts the idea of change into noticing what was unnoticed, where what was unnoticed was not the grounds of change itself but the various things which now become visible, given the security of those grounds. The unnoticeable becomes not what lies covered-over (as grounds are covered-over by usage) but that which is not seen in the most concrete sense. This is to say that the unnoticeable shifts from the forgotten (in a Platonic sense) as in the forgetting of one's responsibility as a speaker, to that which is blocked from view. Only in such a world can travel be seen to

[11] M. Heidegger, *On Time and Being*, trans. Joan Stambaugh, New York: Harper and Row, 1972, p. 57.

change, for in this world it restores one's view (one's eyesight) by putting him in a position to see. The 'change' that travel introduces is then only intelligible through the idea that there is something to see and travel accomplishes this by putting one in a position to re-cognise this possibility.

However the possibility of this recognition is a parametric feature of the human in that the unnoticeable is before our eyes all along as that which grounds and prefigures speech. As an icon for the co-existence of speech and language, to re-cognise the unnoticeable requires no concrete movement, for its recognition is not an analytic effect of movement but a parameter of thinking (and thinking is independent of movement).

This is not to say that movement will not *cause* persons to think in certain situations, but rather: the claim that travel educates equates thinking and moving analytically. Such an identification is only possible in a world in which adequate thinking is seen as an emancipation from the perspective of place—of concrete position—and this is a modern world. The modernity of this world can be seen in the fact that the version of adequate knowledge which it produces is a version which treats observing as knowing and which sees viewpoint concretely as lack of access to observables rather than as commitment. Thus, travel changes only in a world where noticing and observing are taken as synonyms for knowing, where dialectic becomes converted into the method of sheer movement, where the extensive activity of changing places becomes the way to command a view rather than the intensive action of understanding what it is to be anyplace.

Dialectic makes reference to the fact that knowing is independent of place and that to address sources of speech and language is to involve oneself in an engagement whose eternality makes irrelevant the particularity of any one place. Where movement may serve as an occasion or stimulus for such engagement it need not: the fact that dialectic is a human parameter recommends the irrelevance of movement as method.

Movement becomes method in a world in which observation is the paradigm of knowing and when learning requires being present and having visual access. Travel becomes educational in such a world because it makes what is observable accessible by liberating the person from ignorance (but here ignorance is re-defined as not having access or not being present).

150

The connection between movement and education is grounded in an ideal of knowing as experiencing: the experience is symbolised in the activity of noticing what was unnoticed where the grammar of notice-ability makes reference to the idea of being present to (seeing with the eyes, seeing for oneself). Whereas dialectic addresses the grounds of this conception of experience itself, the modern version assumes the connection while using it as a resource of speech. This resourceful use of the conception of experience recommends a radically concrete notion of the 'what' that is known as the new. Of course, we see this emphasis on the newness of the experience to reverberate as an essential feature and ground of the positive world of inquiry; the experience symbolised through the method of travel has its equivalents in the notions of news, data, and findings which are the cornerstones of research.

To say this then, is to say that the world which supports travel as a method for creating intelligible knowledge is a metaphor for the world which science creates as its ideal. It is a world which assumes the identity of knowing and observing, which sees the impediment of being stationary, which equates real change with the movement of commanding a view, and with exposure to the experience of the new.

Movement educates by emancipating a person from inexperience (from innocence) and this is possible only in a world where being in one place is seen as ignorance. This idea is itself only intelligible in a world where self is understood in a particular way. One who remains in one place is formulated as an impotent isolate because this world fails to offer a strong notion of self as a conversation within the soul. It is consequently impossible to see self generating real learning for itself (in a way that includes assimilating the myriad encounters of a world inhabited by dialectically opportune others) because one can only learn when one experiences, and to experience is to move constantly into and out of new positions. The source of stimulation is identified externally and dialectic involvement is reformulated as the most concrete kind of tripping rather than as an internal conversation.

We can understand the modern obsession with ideas like solitude and boredom as pains to be relieved (and in a corollary way the ideas of sophistication and perspective). For the world in which observing, experiencing, moving, and positioning

151

become icons of knowing, and methods for achieving knowledge is also a world in which being in one place is terrifying (boring) and where being able to change places is joyful (sophisticated, emancipating).[12] When place is identified as the crucial source of stimulation, the one-ness of a place symbolises sameness and repetitiveness. Since it is impossible to conceive of energy originating internally in this world, this view of self becomes transformed into an image of the concrete, oppressed ego. In this way, the modern world loses its hold on a dialectical view of self as a playful productive agent.

Similarly when learning is linked to the experience of what is present, the other becomes the source of creative exploration, but here other is limited to an identification with the experience of place. Whether it is the Acropolis or the Prado, a sunset or custom, this feature of the site becomes the occasion for re-collecting what is eternally collectable anyplace. When the traveller accredits travelling as the paradigmatic occasion for collecting himself it is only because he sees his essential humanness passively and fails to recognise the eternality of his collaborative dialectical possibilities. What the traveller fails to recognise is that he is essentially a dialectical creature and that dialectic is not limited to any one place.

Travel is nihilism in that its free speech—speech unconstrained by a language which could ground it—is free of commitment, more precisely free in its commitment to nothing. It is thus at once innocuous (babble, mere movement) and devastating (lonely). As one is unconstrained, committed to nothing, one is surely alone, without ground. Whereas we can think of solitude as being *by* oneself in that one stands back from community and thereby examines the possibility of his unity, loneliness is to fail to make community analytically possible by forgetting that speech needs a ground. Travel as 'escape' is travel as pain, a response which cuts off source, ground,

[12] In fact, one could read the history of western civilisation as it is usually written (e.g., in the decline of feudal society and the rise of bourgeois civilisation etc.), as an icon of this growing sophistication. This is because if one wanted to read this history in that way one could see it as a hymn to the growth of a travel world, which of course is grounded in the modern notion that freedom is equivalent to moving or being able to move. Discussions of learning, of socialisation, and of cognitive growth can also be seen in this way in that development is made equivalent to the accretion of externals.

authority. Solitude, by contrast, is to suffer pain by examining one's fetters in terms of the origins which produce pain. To travel is to forget why we have the pain in that it excludes all but the pain. Pain is thus unintelligible except as a state, something to fear. Although some have said that travel is a search, we can see how it is only a search for relief and in this respect it cannot be a solution.[13]

The traveller, then, is passive (he does not seek to stand by himself) and uncertain (without connection). The traveller's pain is a display of the absence of will, for the traveller seems to exchange one state (pain) for another (pleasure) and thus ignores what would authorise his pain. To treat pain as the matter is to forget whatever authorises the *issuance* of pain. It is in the issuance, the source and not the state, that we can understand the pain, the person, and thereby transform pain and movement into suffering and change.

Travel, an activity which reifies change as movement, self as site, development as encounter, and suffering as pain, is a most conspicuous expression of modern social theory. What is more radically the mark of modernity than the pain of everyday endeavour, and what theory is more modern than the kind which achieves the reification of life's suffering as the existence of pain ? The concretisation of self and consequent identification of coming to know with an exchange of place presupposes a nihilistic actor as the paradigmatic social participant. Self as the site in which other can appear makes men and the social incapable of themselves producing a transformation, a change, except as that transformation is induced by externals, by what is viewed. The actor becomes a receptacle of what is there to be noticed, the self a collection of those pleasures and pains which mark the notice of some thing. To be alive comes to be the existence of states, to be dead to be incapable of notice, and self-expression the equivalent of cries of pleasure and pain. It is a sheer peopled world, an existential world, and in this sense the most factual of worlds, a world exclusively inhabited by words, people, things.

---

[13] We are not making a practical moral suggestion here: whether one should seek relief of this sort in everyday life is not an issue. We simply want to provide for how we might understand such an act.

7 ART

Art is art in so far as we can recognise that artistic activity shows some rule which is required for it to be called art in the first place. Even to be rejected, the artist's work must be seen to be an attempt at art, whether it turns out to be good art, poor art, successful art, innocuous art, or whatever. This is to say that it must be a display of the activity called art and can only be given that interpretation according to rule rather than willy-nilly. What we recommend here, just as we have concerning other analyses to this point, is that art is an activity which collects, as its way of proceeding, its own distinctiveness. It can thus serve as another vehicle of analysis.

We begin Part I with the notion that for art to exist it must be seen that art (the artistic thing) and art's concrete sources (its producer, its subject-matter, its technology) are different. Art is made possible as an activity by being distinguishable in its works, in that one can (must) see the art independently of the artist, of history, of school. After suggesting that this provides art's identity, we then go on to depict the fundamental

154

grammar of art, as well as to address art's possibility as a form of life.

I. THE RULE OF ART IS ITS CONCRETENESS

One reason for starting by making reference to rule is to isolate the idea in so far as it helps us to see how topics are generated (art, science, snubs, etc.). In coming upon the concrete,whatever it eventually turns out to be, we ask how this thing is to be taken, and it is by rule that we decide. We ask such a question, for example, when faced with something perhaps 38 cm. × 51 cm. that has various splotches and lines and colours. How we give attention, and how attention is transformed into understanding in the sense that we locate the relevance of the thing, recommends to us that we are seeing whatever we see. This is not to quest for other objects, of course: we do not give attention simply by looking at other features of an environment and then through the accretion of 'facts' about that environment automatically come to a conclusion. It isn't analytically informative to know we are in a museum, say, or a concert hall, or a supermarket. Rather, we must call on some rule by which the thing can be transformed into a possible course of action without recourse to other phenomena which would require at some point the same kind of decision. Whether correct or not in our initial assessments, whether we gain agreement or not from others, the world sets up a scheme of possibilities that are manifested by that scheme and in no other way. The surrounding 'facts' about particular paintings, the agreements and disagreements and so on, are themselves first contingent upon a rule of relevance such that they can be seen *as* this fact, or agreeably that, or disagreeably something else.

The rule of art is that what we see enclosed in space or sound is nothing but itself, i.e., it is not to be confused with whatever else than itself it brings to mind. There is no 'operationalism' in art in the technical sense—no decision to treat the event seen (heard) as synonymous with the event represented, as in science. This understood, we can also understand that art need not 'represent' anything whatsoever: the reality of art is in no way contingent upon its connection with something else that is real. This is quite different than, say, everyday life, where to be a

155

L

'husband' requires a wife for one thing, and for another, that
the idea of marriage be available. In science, it is not Galileo's
incline that is itself the essential feature of his work, but its 'uni-
versality', i.e., the notion of gravity (weight?) that 'explains'
the behaviour of objects on the incline. Other kinds of activity
trivialise the concrete, whereas art preserves it. Although art
may be treated as if it can recapitulate things, it need not do so,
and indeed is no longer art when so treated. Art is certainly
never the things it recapitulates. It does not literally reproduce
or copy anything, the way an experiment is thought to reproduce an hypothesis.

Thus, to see the thing before us as art requires that we see it
as something other than the kinds of referential description we
attribute to statements in epistemology ('The king of France is
bald'). The sense of 'The king of France is bald' is its claim to
describe something in the world other than itself. But surely
El Greco, Van Gogh, Warhol, all realise that although there are
Cardinals, sunflowers and Empire State Buildings, which have
a life of their own, just as kings of France do, paintings of them
exist independently of them, in so far as the 'validity' of the
paintings is not contingent upon that life. Art doesn't represent
anything other than itself, if only because the materials of art
do not have to exist. Art is not 'practical' in so far as it needn't
attend to existentials to be art. (Whether in not doing so it is
good or bad art is irrelevant here.) Art is neither the concrete
source of the thing seen nor a facsimile of that source. Art is no
more to be identified with its stimuli than with the persons
producing it. We expect that those who see El Greco's Cardinal
will distinguish him from Cardinal——. Van Gogh's self-portrait
is not Van Gogh, it is his self-portrait. If art's power is art's
freedom, we can see now that this freedom derives from its
independence of things, if by things we mean something
(anything) other than art to which art *must* be responsive. In
particular, art's independence resides in the rule that we are to
see it for its own character. The rule, cryptically put: See *it*.
Science is meant to make reference to things—to subject matter,
to ideas, to methods—external to the vehicle. Art cannot be a
vehicle at all, since its character reposes in features internal to
itself. Do not expect to see art describe something and thus to
be able to assess art by addressing its fidelity to something
external to itself. Another way of saying this is that art is

faithful only to it-self and herein lies its radical concreteness.

This integrity is so pervasive that it works even between
kinds of art. There is, for example, a novel by Bernanos called
Diary of a Country Priest, and a film by Bresson called *Diary of
a Country Priest*. Bresson could, of course, simply have filmed
the novel, which in our terms would have been to make the
film represent the novel the way the statement 'The king of
France is bald' represents the king of France. But in this case
he would have been making, in effect, a documentary about
filming novels and thereby confused the source of the film (the
novel) with the film. Such a film would have required that
Bresson be representationally faithful to the novel in the sense
that whatever the related character of events that appears in
the novel (the dialogue, the serial ordering of behaviour, etc.),
that character be transposed onto film by actually showing
those things through the behaviour of the actors and camera.
Needless to say, this is a very popular version of the filmed
novel, but it is a version which either violates the rule for art
or else is itself not an accurate version of what is being done in
the filming of novels.

Bresson, on the other hand, does not make a film that is
merely an illustration of a text. The novel is noted for its
visual possibilities and description, and the conversation of its
characters has in many places the texture and rhythm of dialogue. Yet it is precisely these points Bresson omits from his
film, while at the same time he claims to be utterly faithful to
the novel. How can this 'paradox' be treated? By what principle can we come to understand that Bresson can intentionally
ignore visual and dialogistic aspects of the novel in order to
make a film? We can understand this only by seeing Bresson
as one who in doing his film is asserting the concrete distinctiveness of the film from the novel, thus showing his analytic
understanding of the rule of art. Otherwise—if he merely took
over all the easily filmic features of the novel—he would be
acceding to the 'representativeness' of the novel by his movie,
the criteria for which would then require something like
matching the two in a quasi-scientific assessment. That movie
would be a report of something observed (the novel) and for its
fulfilment would require the viewer to assess in some way the
veracity of the film as report. Bresson does not do anything like

this, however. He grounds his film on the essential distinctiveness between his film and its source elsewhere. What Bazin calls the 'amazing paradoxes' in Bresson's film thus become intelligible, given the understanding: (1) That films are not novels; (2) This is what Bresson is filming in his refusal to illustrate in the film *Diary of a Country Priest* the text of the novel *Diary of a Country Priest*. The refusal *is* the film. Note too that it is not merely that films in general are not novels in general—films are not simply films, either, if by that we mean their possibility as art resides in what various films can be seen to share. Of course we collect films together and segregate them from the collections called painting, music, and so forth. Home movies are films and make no claim to art. If they do, we must still decide on a basis other than that they are films. Collecting 'arts' according to media is merely technical, like gathering up all the people in Detroit, or all the events in 1973. They have no analytic status in so far as we do not need to understand those principles of collection in order to understand their individual members as works of art. Their artistic possibility is contingent instead upon their concreteness, upon the rule that states see *it*, not what it represents.

What we are asserting here is that art, along with other phenomena (sex comes to mind), contains the possibility that its things will be concretely distinctive: they may 'share' absolutely nothing with anything else; they may possess at least *something* that is unshared by anything else; these are the matters to which we attend in doing art. Again, it may turn out that Seymour's painting is no more than a pale copy of Pollack, but this is only the concrete result of the rule that we are to see *it*. In the Seymour case, thus, the criticism is based on the rule and thereby confirms it. Without the rule 'see it' one could not assert that it is a pale copy, and furthermore the criticism would carry no sting.

Art draws attention less to removed general programmes and procedures than to its own concrete particulars. In this it is very different from such things as science, social norms, urban families, demography, social institutions, bureaucratic communications, journalism, architecture, language, and so forth. How silly it would seem, for example, to say that Painter A is as 'inessential' to his art as Clerk B is to his organisation. Not that the painter is the thing seen in the art, but rather that we come to consolidate reference to the painting and to the painter because of the concreteness of the work. This is to say that our attention to art is to its concreteness, to the work as a phenomenon. We do not worry about 'contradiction' in art the way we do in morals and the like. It is not a jolt to see a surrealist painting side by side with a cubist one, the way it is when we see a subjectivist act side by side with a relativist one. What we are saying here, then, differs from what we suggested about snubs: whereas we formulate social interaction as a procedure for seeing the analytic similarity among those who are concretely different, in art we are expected to see concrete differences among the concretely different (unless we are art *historians*, art *dealers*, and so on, which is to be an historian or a dealer and not artistic). It is *this* painting *now* which is the thing of interest, however much other paintings seen at other times may have prepared us to see it. This would seem also to be the point of sexual activity—whatever its causes and limitations in biography and social structure, it is to be treated concretely at the time it is done. Ergo the talk of sex, much as it is in art, that some persons 'over-intellectualise' it.

But our discussion is not meant to establish any antithesis, that we are simply to see differences. This would be a rule that clearly makes what we see now contingent upon what we had seen before, only in a reverse direction (we would be asked to see differences rather than similarities). Rather, it is that we are to see the concrete. The rule in art is *focus on the thing itself*. If we use general grounds or formulae to see (read, hear) the thing itself, they are secondary, subservient, background material at best, inessential to the art however they may shore up opinion. New Criticism in literature was on to this. Its aim was to preserve the character of the work by treating it, in its own terms, independently of its history, context, or social circumstance. We might say here by way of juxtaposition that other forms of criticism, say art history as it is conventionally practised, takes the art out of history. It does so by making art contingent upon a foreign principle, and in a very powerful way: it violates the rule 'see *it*' by submerging the thing in a course of extraneous events (the course of events becomes the necessary ground for seeing the thing). There is nothing wrong with doing history, of course, so long as it is recognised that it is not art. Art's concreteness is of interest in history only in the service of the general. In art, on the other hand, the general is of interest only as it serves the concrete. It is possible to imagine forms of revolution without instances, for example, and still maintain one's grasp of the idea of history. But it is not possible to imagine forms of art without instances, and maintain one's grasp of art. Art is concrete, palpable, an accretion of specifics. History, on the other hand, is only *made up* of the concrete— its fundamental character is what the concrete represents as a course of events such that the concrete is transformed into an instance or model of that course.

Should we say, then, that there can be no 'examples' in art, only works ? Should we say that when we talk of art as examples we have transformed the art into something else ? (Again, there is nothing wrong with this so long as we are aware we are doing it.)

Thus, art works—novels, paintings, poems, music—need not coincide with other artistic events. This gives rise to the 'chaos' of art, which is produced by the rule of the anarchy of works. In the most peaceable of times art remains concretely chaotic, and this is the point, not that art 'interprets' the world best in times of social chaos. Conversely, bureaucracy can only be described as an activity meant to standardise things by ridding them of the artistic import of concreteness. Art is *fundamentally* concrete and thus each thing can be both palpable and discrete. (It is perhaps obvious here that the banal claim of art's uniqueness can be rescued by thinking instead of its concreteness.) It is to this aspect of the world we are expected to give attention if we are engaged with its artistic character. The trouble with formula art is that it prevents seeing its concreteness. This trouble suggests that art is the antithesis of bureaucracy and other sorts of conventional sociological activity. Clerks are clerks in an exactly opposite sense to the aphorism a rose is a rose. The former identifies the actor in terms of his common properties with other actors. The latter identifies the rose as needing nothing extraneous to itself for its intelligibility.

Art is what it is. Unlike science, art realises the concrete by showing itself as itself—as its self sufficient source and ground— without turning away to sources (things) that are external. Art is free from the things that it can be seen as imitating because in producing itself art replaces what it imitates. Art's realness is grounded in its freedom from what it imitates because its very capacity to imitate, which is its productivity, constitutes its superiority. Art's reality, its freedom, consists in its productiveness: in replacing the things it imitates it produces itself as inimitable; in making it-self, it-as-maker shows its self sufficiency. Art's very insularity is the source of its power. In creating itself art shows it does not have to be parasitic because it is life-giving, it makes it-self and the rule 'see it' refers to this capacity of art to generate it-self. In generating it-self art becomes independent rather than dependent; when this capacity is seen as the source, ground and essence of art we can understand its concreteness. 'See it' means see the product as a display of its own self-organising potential—as self generating and self-sufficient praxis.

In summary, the rule of art is to see its concreteness. This is what makes art possible, whether in any particular case one 'succeeds' in finding it or not. This is not to say that art is unorganised, without a tradition, or, simply, innovative (whatever that means)—it is not to invoke the bromide of playing tennis without a net. Nor is it to say that art is exclusively preoccupied with the new. On the contrary, art does have a rule and that rule is the concrete. It is thus distinctive in its own right, as we have suggested by comparing it very briefly with bureaucracy. To be sure, there are schools of art, art oeuvres, and so on, and these are categorisations that require seeing instances of art as more than just themselves such that they can be collected with other instances. But we shall argue that these categorisations are based less upon the rule of art than on the grammars of art, of which there are not an infinite number and can thus serve as a collecting standard; or alternatively, upon other activities in other forms of life which take art as their materials. Before coming to the grammar, however, it is important that we support the efficacy of the concrete rule of art by contrasting art with other activities that proceed under very different sociological auspices.

II. CONTRASTS BETWEEN ART AND OTHER KINDS OF ACTIVITY

Science, common sense, sociology, and other forms of non-artistic activity are organised to solve problems. Science clearly requires some notion that scientific practices can solve for the world those questions the world presents to scientists. Everyday activity, too, requires that we put our questions to the world in a way that permits us to seek solutions and thus dissolve the problem that originated in what we saw. Social organisation is a praxis, say, to solve the (analytic) problem of Hobbes' war of each against all. Common sense, according to Schutz, exists to solve the problem of reflexivity by ignoring it. Solutions to problems of course, get rid of the problems.[1]

Thus Hobbes produces the idea of rational humans giving up their sovereignty to the state in order to solve (his problem of) the war of each against all; Society 'solves' the problem of randomly behaving individuals in many sociological theories; 'social facts' are meant to solve the observational-measurement problem of the overarching abstractness of society *vis-à-vis* the individual; social classes solve the problem of an organised (single) collective that at the same time re-collects itself into several collectives and so on. Each of these solutions serves to ground the concrete behaviour we see in the analytically offered collective (classes, society, etc.) which is then treated (by the analyst) as the source of that behaviour. The behaviour we see, in this case, is only representative of its source, of its collectability within a constellation of memberships. That is, we formulate the behaviour we see in such a way as to make it representative of its source. In this way the sociologist sees individual acts as the identity of the social sources of those acts. In this way the art historian sees 'The Old Guitarist' as having the identity of a blue period.

This is to say that we come to understand incidents in the worlds of everyday life and science and sociology and art history by making those incidents represent the forms of life in which they can be located. Their problematic concreteness

---

[1] By solutions we do not mean, with regard to sociology, that those solutions are empirically consensual. Whether they are empirically held or not, for example, so-called conflict theories in sociology are solutions which permit those holding them to understand the world in the sociological domain, and the question is thereby solved in the sense that the discipline is organised to solve the problem of opacity in social structure by describing its origins and behaviour. This description (conflict) rids us of the problem in so far as it provides a way for coming to terms with whatever the solution recommends.

is transformed into a solution by, in effect, ridding them of their concreteness—by seeing them in terms of their auspices. Thus lovers no less than spouses come to be intelligible by formulating them within the games by which they come concretely to be no more than exemplars. We all have a pretty good idea of what lovers are (not) only by seeing concrete activities through a set of lover auspices. *That* lovers are possible is never questioned, the trouble at hand being solved—even unhappily— by consulting some standardised collection of rules by which the present concrete act is transformed into an exemplar of the social typification and thus into sociological action. Art, on the other hand, preserves the concrete by confirming that it can have an independent existence. That art *is* standardised at any particular point in real time, or the actual world, is in no way necessary for art to occur.

III. STYLE AS GRAMMAR

To this point, then, we have art as an activity organised around the rule that art does not produce representative exemplars of its own community. In other words, art does not re-present community but displays the collectability of eros and genesis as the erotic attachment to becoming. Whatever the possibility of a concrete assembly of artists, paintings, orchestras, libraries, art itself is not dependent upon being so assembled. There must be real artists, of course; there must be paper to print words upon, gut to make strings from, halls to hear music in; but we do not want to confuse the analytic with the concrete, and by community we mean a web of related standards such that those standards are both distinctive to the activity and essential to the acts for their sense. The 'meaning' of a work of art is (partly) its concreteness. The 'arrogance' of a song is precisely its claim not to need any general auspices to exist, only itself. Songs are not indebted to genre for their existence in the way, say, people are indebted to society for theirs.

But—and this will relieve those whose impulse to this point has been to cull examples like 'symphonic form', 'iambic pentameter', and so on, as refutations of art's concreteness— art is not exhaustively concrete. Art cannot be understood, nor done, nor described solely by citing the rule of concreteness. The

163

identity of art, surely, resides in the completeness or concreteness of the thing itself, but it is also characterised by a grammar such that the concrete can be methodically accomplished or done. This grammar, in the arts, is style. The method by which art is generated is style. Style as the eroticisation of becoming, identifies grounds as the successful accomplishment and eroticises collecting as the telos of speech.

To discover that we are seeing a painting requires, for one thing, the rule of concreteness. To see that the object has been *produced* in a certain way and is thus a painting, we look for a style, which eliminates the accidental or circumstantial from possibility as art.[2] In the latter sense, we see the thing not only concretely (as with a rock in a field) but also as an intention. In art the rock has, somehow, been placed there, and the method or style by which this is done is art's grammar. It is art's grammar in so far as we recognise that at this point we are dealing with a claim to art—it is a grammar because we have located the 'relevance' of that with which we are faced. Thus, in general, art is finding a method for producing the concrete. Here is the place for formula in art, in the sense that it locates for us the idea that art can be done. In many respects, the style 'minimal art' is a style that takes style as its subject, i.e., it produces a question about the threshold between art and accident. What if the rocks in the field had been placed there?

So art does, finally, produce a 'problem': to display (see, hear) an intention in the concrete. The solution: style. Style

[2] 'Style is the means of communication, a language not only as a system of devices for conveying a precise message by representing or symbolizing objects and actions but also as a qualitative whole . . . suggesting diffuse connotations and intensifying associated or intrinsic effects. . . . Style is a concrete embodiment or projection of emotional dispositions and habits of thought common to the whole culture.' Meyer Schapiro, 'Style' in A. L. Kroeber, ed., *Anthropology Today*, Chicago: University of Chicago Press, 1953, pp. 304–5. While this characterisation may serve the interests of art history it raises certain difficulties for us by presupposing that it is a characterisation of *artistic* style. There is nothing in the description which generates art as the purveyor of the style, and so we can just as easily think of various 'concrete embodiments' which would fit the characterisation but would not be called art, e.g., friends talking to one another, a political assassination and so forth. It omits the specifically erotic intention we address on the following pages.

is the grammar that permits us to see in the concrete an intention ('intelligence' in the parlance of art criticism) rather than accident (the rock in the field) or sheer circumstance (a man pleading for his life). Style, then, generates its own tension with the chaos of the purely concrete. If the chaos of the purely concrete can be seen to have been intended, that chaos is in some sense solved in that it can be formulated (as art). This is precisely the challenge of minimal art. But it is not restricted to minimal art. It always a challenge in art to see art, because we are expected to attend to the concrete thing and then decide anew if we are attending to art. The concrete, only contingently art, is transformed (or not) by the presence of style.

Style permits us to see the intention in art by displaying that intention as the eroticisation of genesis; genesis is eroticised when it is seen as an end in it-self—when, as it were, the distinction between the Beautiful and the Good is obliterated. When Baudelaire says life is chance and art is necessity we understand this as a way of affirming the intentionality of praxis as beautiful because it organises it-self (by being what it is) rather than by living off what is external to it. To attach one self to genesis as an end is to identify Becoming with the Good; style is a way of seeing the intentionality and hence freedom of such an attachment. It is the life-giving power of genesis as displayed in style that permits us to see the gaiety and enthusiasm of art, because 'style' is the method through which we re-cognise art's freedom from things external to praxis as its essence, ground, and power: its power to create itself as a life outside of life. As a life outside of life it is an eternal and self sufficient domain.

Style makes reference to the ways in which the source of art lies in its freedom from external things and therefore, in intention, which is the affirmation of this freedom; in this way, style displays the erotic attachment to this freedom itself as the source and end of the activity which is art. Art's freedom and eternality resides in its erotic attachment to intention as the source and ground of its productivity. Art's love is exhausted in the activity of arting; art arts as a display of the self sufficiency and freedom of the spirit.

Thus, art makes a difference by repudiating what is different from art. Art repudiates what art does not need to art on the grounds that what is external to this need for its own praxis is not beautiful. Art loves only what it needs, which is to say that it loves its freedom as the re-production of spirit and intention. Art sees everything external to it (to intention, spirit) as ugly because it identifies ugliness with chance, with the fortuitous upheaval introduced when intention relaxes, and only art is beautiful because its creativity affirms its necessity (that art can organise its arting if it concentrates). The beauty of art is that it is what it is—it makes itself—and thus, stands as an icon of the intention which calls it into being. Style is art's method for showing that the difference it makes is controlled neither by God nor things, but by it-self. Art exhausts itself because it continually (re-) produces it-self, it continually asks of it-self that *it* and it alone make the difference it is.

Because art demands of it-self that it constantly make a (its) difference between arting and everything else, it is constantly driven to differentiate its own arting from all other occasions of art. Art must not only display the intentionality which is independent of things external, but each display of even this must affirm its difference from any other display which would join it with history: its social conditions, and so on. The concrete and idiosyncratic affirmation of freedom marked by the display of intention requires the very activity of arting to be unprecedented. The concreteness of art is seen in this: that style announces the freedom of intentionality, but intentionality requires each occasion of arting to be free from history as well as things; each occasion of arting is so completely historicised that it is free of history.[3]

Each display shows itself as different from *any* display by reorganising its genesis as new, as unprecedented. The newness of art consists in its effort to originate itself on every occasion and so, every occasion of art is a particular re-birth of art that must appear as an instance of genesis without generation. Because art produces it-self, its every production must be unprecedented, for it is exclusively an unprecedented production

[3] This is the form or style of art, whatever the particular kinds of expression that art may stress in various historical periods. Whereas art historians discuss style as 'the intrinsic meaning of the work', we prefer to treat style as 'the intrinsic meaning of art'. The former treats the artistic identity of the work as secure, which for us is the very issue that is concealed by art history. Cf. Erwin Panofsky, *Studies in Iconology*, New York: Harper & Row, Torchbook edition, 1962, pp. 3–17.

which owes only to it-self. Otherwise art will still be controlled by things, e.g., other works, tradition, etc.

Art represents a peculiar kind of sociability, for in repudiating history and things art must still take its bearings from that which it repudiates. Art tries to preserve what it sees as evil through its praxis of seeing (of making, doing, becoming) and even while unmasking the contingency of ugliness the beauty can only reside in the praxis of unmasking itself. The purity which art shows in its expression is the purity of a disillusion which remains segregated from the dialectical impulse. In repudiating things external to praxis art shows its necessity, its power and freedom; in repudiating history antecedent to its praxis art shows its originality. In its rejection of *both* chance (gregariousness) and repetition (boredom) style opts for solitude and adventure. By enunciating the necessarily unprecedented, style displays the complete and concrete historicisation of praxis as the moment which it is and nothing more. Things are rejected through the creativity of intention and history is rejected through the original rebirth of this display on each of its occasions.

The position of art then, is this: its beauty consists in its power to repudiate words and things by showing the self sustaining creativity of intention to lie in its negation of dependency. Art is free because it negates dependency, and the act of negation announces its independence. The beauty of art is to show the possibility of negation as beautiful in itself. Art's problem is that it takes this as its limit; in showing that man is free art says nothing about this freedom because to speak about it would be to deny it.

So art need not concretely represent anything in the world in the way we used the idea of representation when referring to science and common sense. Art is still nothing but itself, but now what becomes itself is style. So it incorporates itself through style, but it would be a mistake to think that this is the same thing as 'representing' a style in the way a husband represents marriage, or Toronto represents a city (Toronto is still Toronto as well as what it 'shares'). This is so because style is a method of production *in* a thing and not, simply, a category which may or may not be used on an event, in the way marriage and city are categories. Marriage and city are courses of action that can *exist without incumbents*. They are categories in just that sense. But style cannot exist except through its concrete phenomena. No works, no style. Style reposes *in* its vehicle. This is the meaning of our talk, for example, when we discuss the 'invention' of artistic style, in contradistinction to the 'discovery' of, say, stratification or love. Style cannot exist as a mere possibility, but love can be made reference to even when there are no concrete incumbents to fill the category, and so to realise the possibility. We cannot look to 'discover' a style except through its concrete realisations in novels, symphonies, and paintings, i.e., style must have been invented for us to see it. But we can act as if love is relevant, or classlessness, even though the world is impoverished of them, as in romantic prophecies and Utopias.

Think of it this way: we could not possibly say some piece of art was totally without a style and still call it art, but we could say that some behaviour had no category. We undergo the latter regularly, as in anomia, confrontation, meaninglessness. By the same token, we can be disinterested in the method of common sense (its 'style'), even though it has a method. The idea of a society as a normative order introduces us to the idea that possible courses of action may not occur, while at the same time they remain possible courses of action. The idea of style, on the other hand, requires that it exist in its products: that it have instances. Gass,[4] for example, makes reference to the fact that behaviour *can* occur without style (eating). If we were to see eating as art and not just everyday life, we would have to see *in* the eating the way it is accomplished, and thus its style. But we need not see eating that way, and this distinguishes the behaviour of eating from the art of it. (Gass's notion of style leads to some difficulty because he treats activities as means and ends, and style as instrumental means and thus segregated from the ends. We would say, on the contrary, that in art the artistic thing and its style are analytically inseparable. The one can only be done through the other, else the concrete thing is an accident or circumstance [the rock in the field].)

What we have been saying thus far in separating art from accident depends upon a certain distinction between the human and non-human. This is of course an issue in art, largely because the concrete may not be 'human' and thus not art. To see the

[4] William H. Gass, *Fiction and the Figures of Life*, New York: Knopf, 1970.

human requires seeing the concrete as art, and to see the concrete as art requires the human intention manifested in style. The pristine non-human rock in the field needs to introduce the human intention to become art.

In the other direction, with regard to sheer circumstance, the man pleading for his life needs to be rid of his merely exemplary aspect as a display of society's understandings if it is to become art. The recording of this on film, say, would only be to document that society makes it possible to plead for one's life. Just as art fails to be confirmed by the accidentally non-human, the latter suggests art is not 'purely human' if by that is meant just another version of the social. Art is not just another version of the social because its essence is in the concrete rather than the analytic. The idea of 'society' is in no way essential to it because art can share nothing and still be what it is. It need not be seen to share a typified community of common properties, the way the social does. It can be anomalous, altogether puzzling, and contradictory.

Think again of the Hollywood movie that is organised around the attempt to convince us that the story it is telling us is somehow real. The director of such a film, apparently, keeps it uppermost in his mind that there is a real story, or one which could be real in so far as it could occur in society (it is a category presumed by him to be available to members); and at the same time he keeps it in mind that his film is not real in the sense that it is also known in a positivist way to be his construction, supplied through the artifice of the concrete (our way of distinguishing what he distinguished). The way this fellow proceeds is, peculiarly, to use his medium to deny it, i.e., through various kinds of cuts and dissolves he tries to make the fact of the film unnoticed by those who see it. On the assumption that there is an intrinsic segregation of acts in the world from acts on film, he attempts to reduce that segregation by making it unnoticeable. However much one dislikes this brand of movie, it is a style (some call it realistic) that serves to make the artistic claim. That it fails, or whatever, in the eyes of some is only to see the claim for art by seeing the style. This is the joke in Warhol's *Empire State*, a film which simply focuses for hour after hour on the Empire State Building. He is laughing at our expectation that he will make a claim, and that he will make it through a manipulation of his medium as his style.

So too is the idea of style responsible for the reputations of Hawks and Fuller as 'good' film-makers among auteur critics. Hawks and Fuller self-consciously make just this kind of realistic movie, but without seeming to care about making it unnoticeable. If anything, in their casualness they actually point up the noticeable distinction between real social life and the 'fact' that they are making a film. Auteur critics like this because they like the idea of the 'integrity' or 'honesty' of knowingly acceding to the making of a film in precisely the way that the other realist directors do not know what they are doing. In our terms, auteur critics see Hawks as not just happening to make that kind of movie because of what he takes to be the press of circumstances (the audience's wishes, etc.), nor as trying to convince audiences that they are seeing something else and are not at a movie; rather, he *chooses* to do it that way and thus the auteur can say he understands and is therefore executing a style. As an accumulation of such directors' products, these critics can also claim to have found a genre.

Similarly, Gass is a novelist and not a philosopher (he is both by title) in so far as he sees he is dealing with words and not audiences. Again, it is the concrete that must be fashioned, not social typifications. His attention is to what he writes, and he would only be propagandist or business man or philosopher if his object of interest were his reader. His style cannot take shape in his reader. (Needless to say his reader must participate, in that he must attribute style to the object; if you prefer, we can change the terms but not the principle by saying that the reader must see the style in the object and not in himself.) The interest in words requires that he devote them to a style, such that his words in novels be distinguishable from his words in conversation. In the latter, the words come to be sensible—a course of action—only by invoking the socially organised typifications of society in a way that makes the words examples of that society.

Style, then, is to see the method of production. But it is to see the method of production *in* the concrete object, not as a separable procedure. A style doesn't 'exist' (though it can be discussed) except as a feature of the work. Similarly, the work doesn't exist as art except by the incorporation of style. It is not just working with materials like paints or brasses or some such thing that is characteristic of art (in so far as this working

170

is supposed to implicate human intent), since that is what happens in building stone walls, coiffing hair, and making automobiles. In these latter cases we can choose to ignore the method of production and still grasp the character of the object—climb the wall, brush the hair, drive the car. (We could even appreciate their 'beauty', something that is in no way limited to art, any more than the ugly is excluded from art.) Although these objects and products are assembled, the method of assembly is inessential to our grasp of them. Without such a style in art, on the other hand, we are back to the rock in the field and the man pleading for his life. Though perhaps potentials for art, they have not been worked through a style and thus have no status whatsoever.

IV. FORM OF LIFE

We have suggested that the rule for art is to see the concrete artistic object, and that the grammar of art is style. In art the one infuses the other so that both together can be seen to be a claim for art. Because art's relation to the idea of a form of life is unusual if not surprising, it will be necessary here to review certain analytic ideas and their application to other kinds of activity before we can examine art in this respect.

Recall that bias comes to be an activity that is also a course of social action by analytically placing bias in a form of life, namely in positivism. As we saw that bias is one move in a positivist game, we not only gave it a recognisable identity in its own right, but also showed how it is an enforced and concerted practice in that we provided it with a set of standard auspices. These auspices, in other words, gave us an analytic community of positivism that grounds the claim of bias. We also did this for snubs as a move in an analytic community of common sense, where the latter serves to ground snubs, to make snubs *available* even when they do not happen. In this respect—placing an activity within a form of life—we see the activity as an *election* (though enforced) by showing how it *can* happen and not just providing the means for identifying it when it actually does happen. The form of life gives an identifiable act its status as an analytic possibility for members oriented to that form of life, serves to provide auspices for acts identified by rule and

171

accomplished through grammar. The identity and accomplishment of bias claims needs positivism as its grounds, and the identity and accomplishment of rejected greeting (snubs) needs everyday life as its grounds. What about art?

Whereas the resources of scientific and social actions are located in their own forms of life, art's praxis takes its materials from other forms of life. The pejorative 'art for art's sake', for example, is a recognition that it is subversive to ground a claim to art on materials already transformed into art. Art for art's sake denies the work as an unprecedented re-creation of intention. We don't have phrases like 'science for science's sake' or 'common sense for common sense's sake', and even if we did, would they have the same portent? No, because science and common sense can be for their own sake if by that we mean they can be justified in terms of their own forms of life.[5] 'Art for art's sake' is a formulation in which the possibility of art's having its own form of life is rejected.

In terms of form of life as ultimate grounding for an activity, we might ask 'To what is art faithful?' and contrast this with 'To what is science faithful?' In so doing we ask what sorts of theoretic communities exist such that activities must stay within those communities if they are to maintain their identity. What, if anything, can we find to be the essential and distinctive collective for art?

In science the collective is positivism: a community of like members, all of whom are nature's instruments as messengers. It is to positivism that scientific investigations must be faithful if they are to be received within the community of science. Is there such a collective for art? Or, instead, is it due to the very basis of art, and not just happenstance, that it is so often called esoteric? The 'two cultures' argument, however banal and poorly reasoned, represents of course the presupposition that art has its own form of life (culture). Snow and others tend to

---

[5] Science can be used in other ways: say to solve political problems, but this usage is analytically a political one and thus so is the science. Similarly, common sense may have a place in science—a scientist may be reasonable or a good organiser—but this is simply to say that in the world there are many analytically different activities going on in the same concrete places. The analytic distinctions remain and permit us to recognise in the welter of concrete activities whatever it is that the analytic provides.

think of their argument in the concrete, i.e., (1) There is nothing essentially incompatible between the cultures of art and science; (2) It is therefore the actual people in science and the actual people in art (their training, their energy, their interests) who have created and acceded to the barriers between art and science. We would ask, by contrast, whether—whatever the people of science know in a factual way about art and vice versa—the 'two cultures' exist as two *cultures*, and thus could be said to 'compete' with one another at all, like two runners on a track? And, second, even if two cultures do exist, are they not essentially uncompromisable rather than just factually separated by the interests and training of their practitioners? We have suggested that art is without that kind of culture at all. This absence makes art's runner a phantom competitor and the two activities incapable, not only of amalgamation, but of intelligible collection with one another. Art is not a culture in the way science is, which is to say that art's form of life—its 'culture'—is the demonstration of its freedom from the constraint of anything external.

To look at a piece of science evokes not only its content but science. In fact, it is only through the deep form of life of science that any praxis can evoke the scientific claim of a piece of research. Thus every scientific article formulates itself in such a way as to assure us that we can depend upon the auspices of the positivist community to come to terms with the article. It is not the actual concrete statements of method and content, but the form of life to which those statements make reference that permits us to read the article in a sensible way. In this way, we can add to science the sociology of science, the history of science, the philosophy of science, and the like. While they may seem individually to wrench the science part of the relation, in the sense that an analysis has been performed upon that part, the science can be seen to remain anchored, so to speak, in the form of life from which it has been wrenched. Something of its sources remain, and makes the science retrievable. The thing itself (the scientific research) is in this regard protected by its form of life. The sociology of art, on the other hand, can have nothing to do with art at all, since the art has been made dependent upon something external to itself. That is, the sociology of art is just another case for the display of sociology: audience characteristics, artists' characteristics, the connections between socio-political structure and artistic content, and so on. There is nothing left of the art here, nothing to be returned to art, it loses its character to the point that it is unrecognisable. This is due not to what sociological analysis is, or to what historical analysis is (after all, they do not submerge the activities of science); rather, it comes down to the absence in art of a form of life. Responsibility for this in the analytic sense springs from the absence of a set of deep auspices by which we can reconvert to the artistic from the sociological.

Similarly, we can understand that science does not, like art, have critics who are concretely segregated from science. To do science is also to criticise it, if we think of criticism as assessing the connection of particular works to their putative form of life. Yet art and its critics are segregated. To do art is not also to supply or revise connections between a work and a corpus. There is no regular method for continuous review which is built into the organised activity of art, as it is in science, because art itself does not offer grounds for placement within and without itself. Rather, criticism comes from outside in a discrete and concentrated body of actions that are treated as non-artistic actions. We take this to recommend that criticism is a matter of placing works of art in a game other than their own ('civilisation', 'high culture', 'entertainment', etc.).

Art's particular form of life is not to have a particular subject. Art does not supply any criteria of membership, since it is not a community. Thus, art can take anything—literally anything— as its subject. Although some things are beyond science (art) and beyond everyday life (art), nothing is beyond art (not science nor everyday life). Just as the absence of community makes it easily destroyed, so does this absence enable art to take on everything.

Another way of saying this: if we think of agency as form of life, and of ascribing agency as placing a thing in its form, then art is without agency. Agency is history, it is positivism, it is common sense, it is analysis. We can look for sources here and find them, and describe these sources as different from that which they depict or locate. But the sources of art are nothing autonomous and thus art takes them for itself. The materials of art are history and common sense and science and etcetera, etcetera.

Given that the sources of art fall outside art, we can return

174

for a moment to style and its place as the grammar of art. What style does, as we can perhaps now understand, is to *convert* that which exists in other forms of life, and thus had been no more than a potential material for art (e.g., the course of common sense action 'pleading for one's life'), into a concrete display of art (a styled film). Presumably, the concrete displays of everyday life are examples of the form of life, 'everyday life'. It is the same for particular studies in science, history, sociology. There is no conversion in the latter from one form to another. But this is what happens in art, and it is accomplished through the grammar. By the grammar it lets us know that it is art—it offers up its 'criteria'—rather than whatever it would be in the form of life from which it has been taken.

Art's form of life can also be seen in our talk about art, and in the organisation of art. Terms like 'creative impulse', 'insights of genius', and so forth, can now be understood to emanate from a confused, not to say doomed, search for auspices as forms of life. The emptiness of 'creativity', and other similar terms so overburdened as descriptions of artistic accomplishment, is the inevitable by-product of a search for a form that does not exist. Creativity is in this sense a gloss for a form of life that demonstrates its freedom from constraint through the affirmation of the intentional sources of speech. As we have seen, to show such an intention is to treat speech as renewable on every instance of showing, to free the work from any dependency on externals which would re-focus the instance upon a history or tradition which could ground the instance. Such a ground would conventionalise the instance by organising it into a community of instances and thus obviate the moment as its own genesis. As a gloss, creativity is instructive only in so far as it catches the idea that art is without agency and thus art works are generated out of whole cloth—art is certainly creative if we take the term in this way. We don't place art things in a form of life—at most we see art *through* its grammar. Whatever is creative in this way about a scientific claim, for example, we use to deny the claim. If by creative is meant not in principle reproducible according to the understanding of a positivist form of life, the claim to science is rejected by scientists. In the same way, art cannot be taught to the degree it has no form of life. Naturally. Art appreciation and art history are the teaching of appreciation and of history, not art. To be a scientist one must

175

first be a positivist (know the deep rules of positivism). These can be taught, and taught not just in classes but in everyday life (by learning the democratic ethos, the singularity of nature, about real objects, about explanation). The impossibility of teaching art this way, as opposed to the teaching of line and colour and composition (which would be like teaching mathematics and experimental design in science) is a reflection not of temporary technical primitivism but of the genuine and eternal absence of anything to be taught.

V. ART AND ANALYSIS

Art's rule, 'see it', offers a different recommendation for treating the concrete from the one we ourselves have been offering in all other papers in this book. For any rule, for example that bias is a counter-charge, our analytic task leads us to produce the grounds which can generate the rule, which in bias is positivism. But with art we produce a rule which itself tells us that in our analysis we shall uncover an absent form of life. Not that our analysis will fail in the sense that we cannot find art's form of life, but that as we succeed in examining our understanding of form of life we shall find the life which sustains art to be an anti-form. We do not, in other words, violate our principle of analysis which requires seeking the form of life of a phenomenon. Rather our analysis permits us to see how art is thereby differentiated from other phenomena by being without a feature of activity which is present in those other phenomena. We do seek a form of life for art, and our analysis generates the absence of that kind of form as the form in this case. The rule of art instructs us to look at the thing itself, not to provide for it, not to see it in terms of a set of grounds. When we analysed bias, snubs, and evaluation, our method was always to seek the intelligibility of surface instances through the deep ground which generated them. Art, on the other hand, depends for its possibility only on our seeing it as an instance which shows itself as the affirmation of intention. In effect, the rule of art as provided by analysis requires that we do not supply a deep structure for art, which is to say that art's deep structure is the rejection of such a structure. Art rejects the kind of self understanding which would constrain us to examine anything other than the praxis of self-expression. Art's rationality is that to understand art one must understand it through its concreteness.

This analysis, then, produces first of all a version of how it is possible *not* to do an analysis. We provide a way of not doing an analysis by constructing for art's rule of concreteness ('see it') a form of life which makes the rule sensible. And yet this form of life is organised as a negation of sources external to itself. This is where style fits into our analysis. The form of life which supports style as grammar is our method for constructing the rationality of art's rule. This is to say that 'see it' is intelligible as a rule only if there are no grounds behind it and if it is seeable (style). The world which makes style a display of freedom makes it sensible to look at art rather than at its 'external sources'. It is not that form of life is irrelevant to art. Rather the significant absence of an external form of life enunciates the presence of this absence as a repudiation which is decisive in making artistic activity sensible to us. The only form of life which we (our auspices) can conceive to make art's rule sensible is this negation of the external which affirms the presence of pure intention.

Grammar (style) can be contrasted to mannered art. To see art as mannered is to be unable to stay riveted on the art itself. It is to see the artist in his product, to fail to distinguish between the thing itself and its producer and its other concrete sources. It is just this distinction which is necessary for art, as we have said. Manner, unlike style, contradicts art's rule by directing you away from the thing itself.

Thus far we have style as grammar and no form of life as our version of the rationality of art's rule, 'see it'. Now we want to emphasise that it is *our* version (that it displays our auspices) by suggesting that it is possible to conceive of art in other ways. One other way amounts to analysing art by denigrating it. Art becomes a weak sister to analysis. This approach begins by recognising art's rule, 'see it', but does not construct a deep structure (no form of life) which makes 'see it' sensible. Art is not, according to this view, an alternative to the whole idea of grounds but rather a disregard of them. Art becomes not an affirmation of the kind of form of life it needs, but a lack of any affirmation at all. In other words, the form that repudiates form is made insignificant. This has art say: instead of looking deeply I want to look superficially; or, instead of looking at

177

one thing, grounds, I choose to look at another thing, surface. This conception, of course, makes it possible to see art and science as two different versions of the same old thing, or art as superficial and science as deep, or art as particular and science as universal, or art as whimsy and science as truth, etc., etc. Here the two cultures are not only resurrected—they are ranked.

This version makes it possible to conceive of art's rule 'see it' and, by implication, to conceive of not doing analysis as alternatives, as mere options, rather than deep decisions. Deciding to do art rather than analysis is like deciding to be dirty rather than clean, where it is of course understood that there are certain good reasons for filth. But this version of art does not generate art's rationality at all. Instead it generates art's unimportance. Art seen this way is trivial. For us art becomes rational—that is, 'see it' becomes rational—only if there are no grounds which can provide for what is seen.

If, as we suggest, to do art is to see it, and this amounts to the requirement not to do an analysis, then we now want to say that such a requirement becomes sensible only when analysis is impossible and not a mere option. Art is not, as some modernists would have it, the decision to do it rather than analyse it. Rather, it is a concrete demonstration—or better a demonstration that shows by its concreteness—that *it* can only be done, and hence that analysis is impossible. We make reference to our grounds by showing that any concrete activity can be conceived of as a move in a game. Art is the activity which gets its identity for us by resisting our method—by being conceivable only in itself and not in terms of its game, for its game is non-existent in the way we use the term as the equivalent of form of life.[6] Dealing with art by denigrating it really cannot analyse art at all. It can only generate art by rejecting it as a topic. For this view art is only a matter for disparagement.

Another version of art has already been touched on. Consider again activities like art history, art sociology, art criticism. As we have said, they are to do history, sociology, criticism, but not art. Although all of these activities claim to do analysis, notice a distinction: they can constitute themselves only by

[6] It should be noted, however, that it is our method which generates this resistance, and thus we can say that the method succeeds in so far as it permits us to recognise other methods.

distorting the analytic character of art. Thus, art sociology gets its existence by treating art as if it had social correlates, and art history by treating art as if it could be located in time. These approaches amount to using art's groundlessness not as a topic but as an unanalysed resource for which they attempt to find one or another remedy. Instead of disparaging art's rule 'see it', these versions deal with the rule by making it go away. They can only analyse art by assimilating it to themselves.

One way to summarise the difference between the manner in which these other approaches analyse art and how we do is that their analyses cannot maintain an adequate version of the self–other distinction. They have no idea of 'mixed company', of other as a generative source of self and thus something to be preserved in the mix that is the action of analysis. The One that is community (action, analysis) is achieved by re-collecting the two that are self and other. To treat community as nothing but a concrete one, dropping out the memory of other and thus forgetting how the One is generated, is a de-generate version of the communal possibility, and can only aggrandise self by the denial of other. In the sociology of art and the like, there is no mix, no other. Other becomes self, as art becomes history or sociology, or criticism, by making art's concreteness 'say something' about the externals which art itself has repudiated. If the intelligibility of art is its freedom from dependency, this very solitude makes art susceptible to loss of identity on the occasions of its use by those external to it. The kinds of analysis which produce this loss of art's identity can have no adequate version of other, since they obliterate other in the process of coming to terms with other.

Art as weak sister is a denigration of other by denying art a form of life. Here art's negativity is thought to be simple ignorance rather than a decision to reject. According to this view art doesn't know about other, and that is its weakness. As we have seen, however, art's negativity is not nothing, it is something: it is a way of making itself a self-generating activity. Art recognises the possibility of mixed or external company in its election not to be constrained by the externals which are mixed company. This is denigrated because it is thought not to be an election and hence not a provision for other, i.e., the very issues of mixed company which we have seen as art's rejection of externals is made insignificant. Art says: I recognise

179

mixed company but I will be responsible only to myself. To denigrate such a form as no form is to fail to understand that it is a form, and it is through such a failure that art could be a weak sister (without form). But art speaks of other forms; to think art is ignorant is to confuse praxis with the election praxis displays, a confusion which is itself a display of the failure to be analytic. Art's power is the election to be free from the constraint of mixed company, not ignorance of mixed company. Art chooses to recognise other by repudiating any responsibility to join him. Other is preserved in art by art's choice of self as against other. That other is not a constraint for art is not a happenstance of ignorance but a necessity, and the recognition of art's form requires this understanding.

By contrast, we believe we can address art without either aggrandising analysis or obliterating art, even though the rule of art is the antithesis of the rule of analysis. We conceive of art as being a form of no form, unlike ourselves. This is to say, that when we see art, we see not self but other. When we see art we see a deep distinction between it and ourselves. This point, like all points in this book, is not a concrete truth but a way of making reference to analysis. Who are we such that we can see art as other rather than self?

An inadequate answer to the question of how we can see art as other than ourselves would be that we do not impose our method on others. This is of course symbolic interactionism's palliative for preserving subjectively intended meanings (whatever they are). In our terms, not imposing one's method—if by that is meant not *using* one's method—amounts to refusing to deal with the topic at all. Not to use one's method on art is to refuse to talk about it in any serious sense. This is exactly what those who 'analyse' art only by disparaging it, are doing. Art's concreteness, the fact that style is its grammar, and the fact that its form is no form, were not produced by holding our method in abeyance. They were not produced simply by looking at art while suspending our method. Instead concreteness, style, and form are examples of our method. If we can see art as other, it is only because we have first of all a notion of self, of analysis. Art is other in terms of our conception of self (our ground). The important general point here is that other— the analytic idea of other—can only be constructed by analysts with a definite commitment to a version of self. Thus, those who

180

denigrate art do so because they have no definite commitment to themselves as a methodic accomplishment.

On the other hand are those who are committed to a method, but who think of that method as not requiring the recognition that it is an election which is itself grounded in some kind of rational inquiry. They accede to their method, as it were, and treat it as divorced from themselves. Art history, art sociology, and the like obliterate the distinction between art and themselves by imposing their confused method on art. They make it impossible for art to appear because they insist on treating their analyses as divorced from the grounds which produced them—as divorced from themselves. Their systematic disinterest in what makes their concrete speech possible makes it impossible for them to see art as other than themselves. By thus defaulting on their own grounds, they fail to preserve other.

This point is fairly complex. Consider once more our own analysis of art. If our analysis is read concretely, it also assimilates art to itself. In saying that art has a rule, a grammar, and a form which makes that rule and grammar sensible, we are treating art exactly as we treat every other activity which we analyse. But the crucial point is that the reason for this talk, for this treatment of art, does not, according to our method, reside in the nature of art but in our commitment to analysis. Rule, grammar, and form of life is how *we* have to speak if we are to do analysis. But even art sociology can stand as an example of the deep difference between art and sociology if it is conceived not in terms of what it says about art but how what it says is possible—in other words, if it is conceived in terms of what it says about itself. Other is constituted analytically by remembering how that constitution is produced by one's own commitment.

For us, other can only be seen through the commitment which is not an analysis but which organises analysis as something to be done. Other is re-cognised by thinking back to one's grounds, grounds which are external to any particular substantive analysis like snubs or art and yet which make it possible to do those analyses. Other isn't art, or common sense, or science as we have distinguished them, but that commitment which produces attention to these matters. Other isn't the difference, but that which makes the difference. This is to say that other is not nothing just because it isn't visible (before analysis) nor is it identical with what we have made visible (after analysis). Other is that which organises and grounds the idea of analytic interest. Analytically speaking, other is what makes the difference(s) we have described as art, common sense, and science, not the difference(s) themselves. Other makes it possible to affirm what is as the embodiment of a dialectic tension of commitment. Being our commitment, it is our affirmation. But it is an affirmation which transcends sheer relativism because it is backed by a commitment that is external to the things we analyse, and external to these particular analyses. It is our form.

Just one implication: our work may appear to be solipsistic. We only talk about other topics in order to make reference to ourselves; we see everything in terms of ourselves, etcetera, etcetera. Now it appears that if by solipsism is meant inability to conceive of other, we not only escape the charge but we can turn it on all those who ordinarily would make it.

NAME INDEX

Aristotle, 40
Atkinson, J. W., 26n
Austin, J. L., 23, 27, 40n

Baudelaire, C. P., 165
Bazin, R., 158
Bennett, Jonathan, 35n
Bernanos, G., 157
Bresson, R., 157-8
Burke, Kenneth, 31

Cattell, R. B., 26n
Chomsky, Noam, 7, 29n, 32
Clark, R. A., 26n

Denzin, Norman, 22
Durkheim, E., 23, 69

Freud, Sigmund, 109
Fuller, S., 170

Garfinkel, Harold, 22, 82n
Gass, William H., 168, 170
Gerth, H. W., and Mills, C. W., 29n, 30-1
Goode, W. J., and Hatt, Paul, 51n

Habermas, J., 7
Harré, R., 58, 61
Hatt, Paul, 51n
Hawks, H., 170
Hegel, G. W. F., 132
Heidegger, Martin, 23, 110n, 149
Hobbes, Thomas, 125n, 162
Homans, George C., 23
Hume, D., 28

Inkeles, Alex, 23

Kojeve, A., 132, 134-5, 147n
Kovesi, J., 93n
Kuhn, F. F. A., 96

Lindzey, Gardner, 26n
Lyman, Sanford, 29n

McClelland, D. C., Atkinson, J. W., and Clark, R. A., 26n
Mallarmé, S., 11
Mannheim, K., 59
Marx, Karl, 23, 24
Melden, A. I., 27-8
Merton, R., 96
Mills, C. W., 29n, 30-1

Nietzsche, F., 56, 94, 95n

Panofsky, Erwin, 166n
Parsons, Talcott, 125-6, 128n; and Edward Shils, 50n
Peters, R. S., 27n
Plato, 14, 15, 67
Polanyi, Michael, 104
Protagoras, 23, 67-8
Proust, Marcel, 121-2

Riley, M. W. 50n
Rosen, Stanley, 3

Schapiro, Meyer, 164n
Schutz, A., 162
Scott, Marvin B., and Lyman, Sanford, 29n